THE
POCKET BOOK
OF
CELTIC

By Douglas Beattie

For Keir and Ilsa

Published by Vision Sports Publishing in 2010

Vision Sports Publishing
19-23 High Street
Kingston upon Thames
Surrey
KT1 1LL

www.visionsp.co.uk

ISBN: 978-1905326-97-6

Series editor: Jim Drewett
Series production: Martin Cloake
Design: Neal Cobourne
Illustrations: Bob Bond
Cover photography: Paul Downes, Objective Image
All pictures: Getty Images unless otherwise stated
With special thanks to Jason Hall and John Rae Elliot

Printed and bound in China by Toppan Printing Co Ltd

A CIP catalogue record for this book is available from the British Library

THIS IS AN UNOFFICIAL PUBLICATION

All statistics in *The Pocket Book of Celtic* are correct up until the end
of the 2009/10 season.

CONTENTS

FOREWORD BY
JOHN HARTSON

The five years I spent at Celtic were, without doubt, the best five footballing years of my life. Signing for the club was the best decision I ever made and from the reception on the day I signed in 2001 to my final game against Aberdeen in 2006 I had an amazing, amazing rapport with the supporters.

It's only when you play for the club that you realise what a giant it is. I remember we played a pre-season tournament in America with Chelsea and Roma and there were 75,000 Celtic fans in the ground.

But it's not just the numbers of fans, they are also incredibly loyal – faithful through and through as the song goes. The rapport I have with them continues to this day and I am so grateful for the support shown to me and my family in recent times as I fought my battle against testicular cancer. To receive a letter signed by 10,000 Celtic supporters wishing me a speedy recovery was unbelievable. It says it all about these people and I know I'll 'never walk alone'.

It could all have been so different, of course. As most people know I was on the verge of signing for Rangers. It was all done and dusted and I was ready to put pen to paper, then they said I'd failed the medical because of my knee. When Martin O'Neill got in touch to bring me to Celtic he said, "Unless you've got a hole in your heart I want you" and in five years I can honestly say I didn't miss a single day's training because of my knee.

Everything happens for a reason I suppose. Rangers got Tore Andre Flo for £13 million and I went on to score 100 goals for Celtic, including four consecutive Old Firm derbies, one at the Nou Camp against Barcelona and of course the 30-yarder against my boyhood team, Liverpool, at Anfield in the 2003 UEFA Cup.

That was a rare shot from outside the box. Usually I would just lurk inside it and wait for a chance, which invariably came along with the likes of Henrik Larsson, Chris Sutton and Stiliyan Petrov alongside me. It was brilliant, we were such an attacking force we put the fear of God into the opposition.

I hope you enjoy this cracking little book, packed with all things Celtic, and look out for the re-run of my Anfield goal on page 56.

And finally, for the men reading this, don't make the mistake I did – check yourself regularly. Take a look at the John Hartson Foundation website for further information.

www.johnhartsonfoundation.com

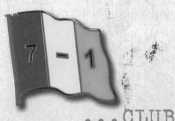

...CLUB DIRECTORY...

Club address:

The Celtic Football Club, Celtic Park, Glasgow, G40 3RE, Scotland

General club enquiries: 0871 226 1888

Official website: www.celticfc.net

Matchday enquiries: (except ticket enquiries) th@celticfc.com

Tickets: 0871 226 1888; fax: 0141 551 4223; homematches@celticfc.co.uk

Visitors centre: 0141 551 4308

Celtic superstore: 0141 551 4231; celticmerch@celticfc.co.uk

Channel 67: 0141 551 4497 / 4227 / 4362; webhelp@celticfc.com

Celtic View: Editorial 0141 551 4264;

celticview@celticfc.co.uk

Fans' Comments:

tictalk@celticfc.co.uk

Corporate services: 0141 551 4366 / 4392;

matchdayhospitality@celticfc.co.uk

Walfrid restaurant: 0141 551 9955

Celtic Supporters Association:

0141 556 1882

Disabled supporters: 0141 551 4351

Celtic Charity Fund: 0141 551 4262

IF YOU KNOW YOUR HISTORY
STRAIGHT TO THE TOP
1887-1929

Celtic is a football club unlike any other.

The great football institutions which emerged from the grimy industrial cities of Victorian Britain tended to be attached to factories, schools and even cricket teams; Celtic represented an entire community.

It was during November 1887 that prominent figures among Glasgow's burgeoning population of Irish immigrants decided they required a team of their own. There was no vanity in this, rather a compulsion to help fill the bellies of the 'needy children' living in the slums of the city's east end.

The inspiration had come from Edinburgh where Hibernian – another side founded by migrants from the Emerald Isle – had been growing in strength. They'd won the Scottish Cup of 1887 and afterwards a senior club official addressed guests at a celebratory dinner in Glasgow, urging the Irish in that city to follow Hibs' example.

Amazingly, within six months – under the careful guidance of men such as the local priest, Brother Walfrid – a patch of waste ground had been made ready for first-class football. On 28th May 1888 Celtic's first side ran out in front of 2,000 people, who cheered them to a 5-2 victory over a Rangers' Select.

Although very much concerned with the welfare of Catholics, indigenous Scots were never excluded. The club's name was evidence of this policy: Glasgow Hibernians, it was felt, held too narrow an appeal, while Celtic was representative of both the Scots and Irish peoples.

The first Celtic team in 1887. In the back row of players, Willie Maley is second from the right

Jimmy Quinn, the brilliant striker who scored a hat-trick in the 1904 Cup final

The new club showed it had no intention of working its way slowly to the top of the game. No less than six of Hibs' cup-winning side were snapped up, a move which soured relations with the Edinburgh outfit for years. Remarkably, in their inaugural season Celtic reached the Scottish Cup final, being defeated in a replay by Third Lanark. However, they did manage to beat the great English side Corinthians 6–2 and, just two years later in 1891, lifted their first major trophy, the Glasgow Cup.

Perhaps it was this immediate success which tempted their landlord into demanding a hike in rent from £50 to £450 per year. This prompted the board to consider moving from the east end, but thankfully another site was identified close to the existing ground. These waterlogged acres were quickly turned into what was viewed then as the best stadium in Britain, complete with cycle track and grandstand. Understandably it was nicknamed 'Paradise'.

Those watching would certainly see a team fit for such an arena. In 1891/92 Celtic took the Glasgow

Cup again, as well as the Charity Cup and the Scottish Cup. The following year their first Scottish League title was secured.

Off the field the directors pioneered changes to the game in leading moves to turn it professional. Celtic had always been prepared to pay their players while the most successful team in the land – Queen's Park – stuck rigidly to amateurism.

The benefits of professionalism were clear: it stemmed the flow of top players heading south to England for higher wages, and helped Celtic secure the title in three of the first six years the league was in place, between 1891 and 1896. This was further proof that the Bhoys were no flash in the pan, but likely to be a real and lasting force in the game.

Boasting the biggest support in Britain and with money pouring in at the gate, Celtic became a limited liability company in 1897. Those in favour claimed to be putting the club on a more secure business footing; others felt deeply aggrieved that the charitable founding principles were being sacrificed for profit.

The years immediately thereafter proved transitional. Cups were won sporadically, but there were also long losing sequences. Then in 1903 the strip was changed to green and white hooped jerseys and out of the shadows stepped a truly special side, the fulcrum of which was Jimmy McMenemy – a gifted playmaker nicknamed 'Napoleon'. Alongside him there was a bustling little striker called Jimmy Quinn.

The Celtic side of 1907/08, now with the famous hooped shirts

Super striker
Jimmy McGrory

It was the brilliant Quinn who notched a hat-trick against Rangers in the Scottish Cup final of 1904. This victory was the catalyst for an unprecedented winning run of six league titles in a row between 1905 and 1910, along with another two national cup triumphs during the same period.

The 1909 cup could also have been added had it not been withheld after a replayed final against Rangers ended in a draw. Fans from both sides lit fires on the pitch and fought with police. It was a sure sign that the poisonous 'Old Firm' rivalry was growing, Rangers having replaced Queen's Park as the main challengers to what the press still called 'the Irishmen'.

The Govan side would have little joy immediately before, during or after the First World War. With Quinn still causing havoc a slip of a lad called Patsy Gallacher was added to Celtic's ranks. Here was a player with such outstanding ability that one commentator described him as: "a man whose frolics on the field were the wonder of the football world".

By 1916 the league championship trophy had

come to Parkhead 13 times. This was more than all the other champions put together and almost twice as many titles as Rangers had managed.

But alas the 1920s ushered in unwanted change. Jimmy Quinn took well deserved retirement and McMenemy was transferred after 18 years' service. Over at Ibrox a much more disciplined regime was installed under Bill Struth, a manager who would dominate the decade with teams built on height and strength, in contrast to the flair that had long been associated with Celtic.

Alan McNair, Celtic and Scotland right back from a 1922 illustration

For Hoops fans there would be still be things to shout about. The league was won in 1921 and 1926, and there were three Scottish Cup successes. Also Jimmy McGrory, a striker without equal, arrived and set about creating new scoring records. Yet those searching for portents would have been right to fret that the fire which destroyed the old main stand in 1929 was ominous.

Presented with FOOTBALL SPECIAL, October 14th, 1922.

OUR FOOTBALL BOYS - No. 8.

Alex McNair
"Celtic"

ALEC McNAIR (Celtic). A household word in Glasgow. Plays right-back, stands 5 ft. 8 ins., weighs 11 st. 10 lbs., has lots of caps, and comes from Stenhousemuir.

BADGE OF
HONOUR

For many decades Celtic played without a badge of any description on their shirts. That, of course, is no longer true today and nor was it the case back in 1888. Then, the very first team to represent the club carried a large green Celtic cross with an oval blood red background on their breasts.

That emblem disappeared from the jersey the following year. It was replaced for a time in the 1890s with a golden harp against a blue background, a traditional symbol of Ireland, which was also used in advertising matches at Parkhead during that latter part of the 19th century.

Over recent decades the four-leaf clover, a good luck charm dating back to Pagan times, has come to be associated with Celtic. It's not clear when and how this was first used, but it's thought it may have been taken from the plaque designed by an early supporters' club; something which reminded board members of the rich green sod which had been brought over from Donegal and placed in the centre circle in 1892.

Celtic green on a blood-red background, the original badge was worn for just one year

What we can say for certain is that it was inscribed onto medals presented to the players back in 1908. These marked their achievements in winning a clean sweep of trophies that season: the Scottish League Championship, the Scottish Cup, the Glasgow Cup

and the Charity Cup. Four leaves were required, since one trophy was mentioned on each.

This traditional symbol of Ireland appeared briefly on shirts in the 1890s, and was also used in advertisements for matches

The clover was also used officially at dinners and on memorabilia during the 1920s and 30s, though never making it as far as the shirt. However, a large green three-leaf version, more commonly thought of as a shamrock, appeared on the team's away kit at various times from the 1920s to the mid 1960s.

In season 1976/77 the double diamond badge of the sports manufacturer Umbro was added. Then a year later, for the first time ever, the four-leaf clover adorned the hoops. The vast majority of major clubs had gone down the route of displaying a badge on their kit. This was Celtic's effort to do the same; an act of modernising which created a design classic at the same time.

A three-leaf clover, or shamrock, appeared on away shirts between the 1920s and 1960s

The badge was altered considerably in time for Celtic's centenary in season 1987/88. The then chairman, Jack McGinn, reinstated the motif which had been used on the first strip, the

Celtic cross. McGinn had tried and failed to discover why it had originally been chosen, but understood its importance nevertheless, since Willie Maley – the Bhoys' legendary first manager – had written a book about the club which featured the same design on its cover.

With a glorious league and cup double won during the centenary celebrations, the crest proved to be highly popular with the supporters and was even used in eye-catching style in a large-scale floral display at the Glasgow Garden Festival.

The badge that appeared on the front of Willie Maley's book about the club…

By the time the next kit was issued, for the 1989/90 season, the now traditional clover had returned.

The emblem would not be altered again until 1995 when, having become a public rather than a private limited company, the words

… inspired the 1987/88 centenary season badge, seen here on Andy Walker's shirt

on the badge were changed from The Celtic Football and Athletic Co Ltd to read simply The Celtic Football Club.

Suggestions from inside Parkhead at this time, that the clover motif should be dropped so that "some sort of Scottish element could be incorporated", eventually came to nothing. This was probably because such a move would have been met with considerable opposition from season ticket holders.

Then, between 1993 and 1997, the crest was displayed in the middle of a white shield – though there was no fiddling with the badge itself.

A single white five-pointed star marking Celtic's European Cup triumph was a welcome addition for the start of the 2004/05 campaign. In the years since the star has remained; turning to black and then gold in the process.

By 1989, the original four-leaf clover had been restored to the badge

An even more obvious reference to the historic win over Inter Milan came in the design of the entire team strip in 2007/08 to mark the passing of four decades since that great day and the triumph of the Lions of Lisbon. The kit was a copy of the one worn that night and featured a woven design on the back with the words 'Celtic 1967' and 'Lisbon'.

THE BHOYS IN SEVILLE

No one could have predicted that the 8-1 trouncing of a little known team of minnows from Lithuania in September 2002 would lead to a fiesta of epic proportions in southern Spain eight months later.

Having been dumped out of the Champions League at the last qualifying hurdle by FC Basle, Martin O'Neill and his men were parachuted into the UEFA Cup. After beating FK Suduva both home and away, they progressed to what was expected to be a much tougher tie against Blackburn Rovers.

There was added spice in that the English side were managed by the former Rangers' boss Graeme Souness. A late goal by Henrik Larsson at Parkhead was the only strike on the night, but when the Blackburn captain Gary Flitcroft kindly informed the press that, "The gaffer said it was men against boys out there", no more incentive was needed. Celtic stormed to a deserved 2-0 win at Ewood Park.

To be playing European football beyond Christmas for the first time in 23 years, Celtic then had to overcome Celta Vigo. Away again in the second leg The Hoops held out for a nervy away goals victory thanks to a tremendous shot on the spin by John Hartson. O'Neill said his players had "created a bit of history".

He wasn't wrong, and they would continue to impress when Stuttgart came to Parkhead in February. His side shook off the loss of an early goal to win 3-1 on the night, without Larsson who had a fractured jaw. Alan Thompson and Chris Sutton both scored early in the return in Germany and Celtic did enough to progress 5-4 on aggregate.

Hartson minds – scoring at Anfield meant so much to big John

Having been written off in each of the previous three rounds they were given almost no hope of beating Liverpool in the quarter-finals. Again the bookies were proved wrong. The Anfield outfit secured a credible 1-1 draw in Glasgow, but back in Liverpool, they were swept away by a side being driven to new heights by their boss.

After the stunning 2-0 win, Neil Lennon explained that they'd been told in the dressing room to "prove to England and Europe that you deserve respect, and that you are worthy of respect and that you are worthy of a place in the semi-finals".

On paper it seemed like the draw for the semis had been kind, The Celts avoiding Lazio and Porto. Instead they would face the traditionally smaller side from Portugal's second city – Boavista.

With the first leg yet again at home, nerves seemed to get the better of everyone and a flat 1-1 draw was played out. Having missed a penalty in the first match Henrik Larsson was on hand to prod the ball home with just 12 minutes remaining of the return leg. That solitary effort was enough to spark raucous celebrations: Celtic were going to Seville for their first European final in 33 years.

There they would take on Porto, managed by a rising managerial star – Jose Mourinho. The captain at Parkhead, Paul Lambert, summed up everyone's feelings by saying the final would be nothing less than, "The game of their lives". What the players and management could not have known was the phenomenal level of support they would receive on 22nd May.

The romantic city in heart of Andalusia had fallen to both the Moors and the Romans in times gone by, but the normally genteel streets lined by orange trees now rocked to the carousing of at least 80,000 happy Celts. Locals were dumbfounded to find bagpipers and men clad in kilts and giant sombreros drinking, dancing and cooling off in fountains. Many came without the slightest hope of finding a match ticket or even a bed – with thousands sleeping rough. There were hundreds of special charter flights and every airport in Spain

El Celtic fan

heard the taunting cries of "You'll be watching The Bill, while we're in Seville", directed at Rangers' supporters stuck at home.

For those who'd only heard of the great deeds in Lisbon and had perhaps wondered if their generation would ever see The Bhoys in such a final, all this was something truly special.

The match was played at the end of an exhaustingly hot day, temperatures were close to 90 degrees. Martin O'Neill, unable to call on John Hartson because of injury, chose as his starting XI: Douglas, Mjallby, Balde, Valgaeren, Agathe, Lambert, Lennon, Petrov, Thompson, Larsson, Sutton. It was essentially a clash of cultures; Porto made their opponents look overly-physical by diving at every opportunity and wasting time. Despite two brilliant goals by Henrik Larsson the final slipped away, 3-2 in extra time. Had Bobo Balde not been sent off late in the game then it may have been different.

There was a sadness that Celtic had come up short on the big occasion, but they'd been beaten by the team which would win the Champions League 12 months later. They'd also gathered many fans both in Seville and beyond; the supporters being showered with awards by the football authorities for their faultless conduct.

When the dust settled there would be the memories of an unforgettable run, some great victories and the party to end all parties. As Seville's director of hospitality said, "The quantity of beer we have sold has never been known before... I don't remember a day when there have been so many non-Sevillanos in the city, not even the final of the Spanish Cup, not even the World Cup of 1982."

Porto's coach, the enigmatic Mourinho, put it another way. "My team played in the UEFA Cup final against a Scottish side – it was Celtic. I've never seen such emotional people. It was unbelievable."

CELTIC COMIC STRIP HISTORY 1

LISBON, 1967... MOMENTS BEFORE THE EUROPEAN CUP FINAL, INTER MILAN AND CELTIC LINED UP IN THE TUNNEL. THE ITALIANS HAD AN AIR OF ARROGANCE...

SEE THEM... ALL TANNED WITH GLEAMING WHITE TEETH...

THEY LOOK LIKE MOVIE STARS!

SUDDENLY BERTIE AULD BURST INTO SONG...

"HAIL, HAIL, THE CELTS ARE HERE..."

...AND THE REST OF THE TEAM JOINED IN. INTER LOOKED ON, BEWILDERED...

...REALISING THEY WERE TAKING ON A SIDE WHICH KNEW THE EUROPEAN CUP WAS GOING BACK TO SCOTLAND.

SO IT PROVED!

PARADISE

Quite understandably the supporters

have always felt a strong emotional tie to Celtic Park. There are many reasons for its special aura, but above all else is the fact that the ground was originally built by the hands of those who would stand on its slopes. Few – if any – other football clubs can match such a labour of love.

It was first constructed on a vacant patch of land next to the Janefield cemetery in the Parkhead district. There an army of Irish volunteers toiled to produce a level playing field of grass 110 yards long by 66 yards wide, surrounded by stands and terracing.

Relations with the landlord were never good and he'd threatened legal action before the first match, having been taken aback by the full extent of the changes being made on his property. Nevertheless the inaugural exhibition game between Hibernian and Cowlairs went ahead as billed on 8th May 1888 in front of 5,000 spectators. It was hardly surprising that a demand for an astronomical increase in rent then led to a severing of relations in 1891.

Fortunately Celtic were able to secure a site across Janefield St, a few

There's always a strong sense of place and history at Celtic Park

hundred metres away. This new location was a quarry
– or 'clayhole' – which had to be drained of water,
with ten thousand cartloads of earth used in the
process. Again, the Irish community rolled up their
sleeves and rallied to the cause. The ground's capacity
– 50,000 rising to 70,000 within a few years – far
outstripped the norm of the time.

It was ready for the start of the 1892/93 season,
complete with a grandstand on the north side and a
separate pavilion located nearby. This latter structure
looked like a large villa and would serve as the team's
base, with offices and a veranda overhanging the
dressing rooms.

The ground was so opulent that senior members of
the English Football League felt Celtic's home was
"far and away superior to any field in Great Britain".

Even empty, Celtic Park
is an imposing sight

Disaster struck though in 1904 when the grandstand was destroyed and the pavilion damaged in a blaze which the *Glasgow Observer* described as a "brief but savagely furious conflagration".

The cost of repairs were put at a dizzying £6,000, but having the luxury of being financially secure Celtic simply replaced the stand with a covered

Archibald Leitch's red-brick facade was given a modernist twist in the 1988 revamp

enclosure and bought the Grant Stand, which a
director had built privately on the opposite side,
closest to the London Rd. That stand lasted until
1929 when it was demolished after becoming unsafe.
Sadly, in the early part of the same year fire again took
hold of the pavilion, sending most of the club's early
records up in smoke.

Celtic called in the leading football architect

Archibald Leitch and asked him to
design a replacement for the Grant
Stand which would become the hub
of life at the ground. This new
structure, commonly known as the
main stand, remained virtually
untouched for 40 years.

During that time there would be
nothing more than piecemeal
improvements which saw four
pylon–like floodlights installed and a
roof constructed over each terracing
behind the goals.

There was also a new roof and
concrete steps placed, for the first time,
in 'The Jungle'. Formally titled the
North Enclosure, this was the
renowned terracing opposite the main
stand which contained the most vocally
partisan Celtic supporters. Dark and
basic it may have been, but it generated
atmosphere like nowhere else.

CELTIC PARK

BUILT: 1892 ONWARDS
LOCATION: KERRYDALE STREET, GLASGOW
CAPACITY: 60,000

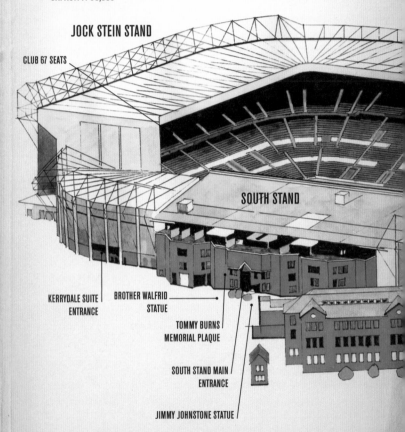

JOCK STEIN STAND

CLUB 67 SEATS

SOUTH STAND

KERRYDALE SUITE
ENTRANCE

BROTHER WALFRID
STATUE

TOMMY BURNS
MEMORIAL PLAQUE

SOUTH STAND MAIN
ENTRANCE

JIMMY JOHNSTONE STATUE

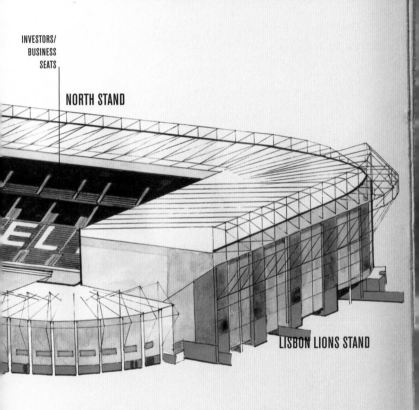

INVESTORS/
BUSINESS
SEATS

NORTH STAND

LISBON LIONS STAND

LONDON ROAD
PRIMARY SCHOOL
(CLOSED 2005)

A major refit was carried out on the main stand in 1971. The structure, which was opened by Jimmy McGrory, had cost £250,000 and could seat almost 9,000 fans. It used state-of-the-art technology to suspend the roof on a giant girder, as if it were hanging on an enormous crossbar.

Then the last remaining part of the Leitch-inspired stand – the red-brick facade – was replaced during the centenary season of 1987/88 by a rather angular modernist creation, complete with tinted glass.

Yet it was an inescapable fact that the once popular old ground – which had been chosen to host religious gatherings, cycling championships, a baseball match and pop concerts down the years – was looking rather dowdy by the late 1980s. With Celtic fans becoming ever-more restive about the ability of the directors to challenge Rangers, the stadium's future became a stick with which to beat the board.

There were farcical attempts between April 1992 and the spring of 1994 to convince the public that moving to an industrial site on the outskirts of Glasgow was the answer. The cost of building this space-age creation in Cambuslang was put at £100

million; the kind of money the directors could only dream of raising.

That didn't stop the plans being peddled in official publications as: 'The World's Best Stadium for the World's Best Fans'. As widely suspected, this was simply the last desperate act of men clinging to

With a 60,000 capacity, Celtic Park is now the second biggest club stadium in the UK

power. Eventually the whole thing unravelled in the press and ultimately led to a change in ownership, with the Scots-Canadian entrepreneur, Fergus McCann, taking control.

A year later in 1995, having spent a season at Hampden Park, The Bhoys returned home to be confronted by a very different scene.

A new high-rise North Stand had taken the place of the fabled 'Jungle'. The Lisbon Lions' Stand followed within 12 months; before the stunning re-development was completed in August 1998 with the addition of the Jock Stein Stand.

With a 60,000 capacity Celtic Park now boasts the distinction of being the second largest club stadium in the UK. It is generally-acknowledged to be a magnificent place to watch football – a ground the fans can rightly be proud of – but more than that, it remains a home from home still capable of evoking warm memories of so many of the heroes of yesteryear.

It's still a grand old ground to cheer from

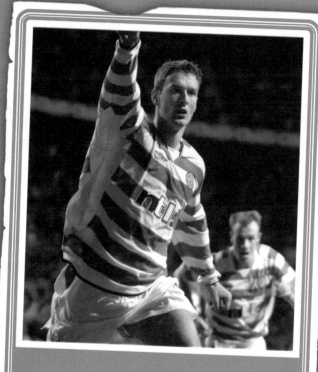

GREAT GOALS

PATSY GALLACHER
1925 SCOTTISH CUP FINAL V DUNDEE

Having drubbed Rangers 5-0 in the previous round, Celtic were not expected to be a goal behind to underdogs Dundee at Hampden.

With the game ebbing away it looked as though the trophy would be heading to Tayside. That was until one of the most unusual and inventive goals ever conjured saved the day.

Fifteen minutes were left when Patsy Gallacher – an impish genius of a dribbler – went on a run, beating several opponents with his usual show of trickery. Slaloming into the box, he was eventually upended just short of the goal line. Then, amid cries for a penalty, Gallacher trapped the ball between his legs, somersaulted the Dundee goalkeeper and landed with his boots tangled in the net.

A fine header from Jimmy McGrory sealed the win but afterwards all the talk was of the outrageous equaliser by 'Peerless Patsy.' Celtic manager Willie Maley summed things up by saying: "It was one of those incidents which had to be seen to be appreciated and it was with difficulty that the Dundee players refrained from joining in the tribute to that wonderful little player."

This supreme act of virtuosity would be so savoured that, nearly a century later, fans still speak fondly of a match which is remembered simply as 'The Patsy Gallacher final'.

NEILLY MOCHAN
1953 CORONATION CUP FINAL V HIBERNIAN

Nearly 120,000 had crammed into Hampden for the final of this knockout competition marking the ascent of the new monarch. Four Scottish sides were joined by the best from south of the border.

A song, which imagined the Queen and Prince Philip dreaming up the tournament, caught the popular imagination at Parkhead. It contained the immortal lines: *"We'll send them a trophy that Rangers can win. Said Philip to Lizzie – watch the Celts don't step in."*

That's exactly what they did. Having had a miserable season, the Hoops came to life, disposing of Arsenal and then Manchester United. In the final they would meet an excellent Hibernian side who were overwhelming favourites.

Again the bookies were made to look foolish. With half an hour gone Neilly Mochan received a pass from Willie Fernie, almost 40 yards out. As he explained, after taking three or four strides the strongly built forward just "hit it with everything". The shot, with his weaker right foot, screeched high into the net, instantly becoming part of Celtic folklore.

This remarkable goal would be a talking point long after his side's 2-0 triumph. Mochan, who served the club behind the scenes for many years, could be found regaling Celtic players with his Coronation Cup exploits even in the late 1980s.

TOMMY GEMMELL
1967 EUROPEAN CUP FINAL V INTERNAZIONALE

An early summer afternoon in Lisbon was the scene of Celtic's greatest triumph. With Inter a goal up and an unforgiving sun beating down to take temperatures above 80 degrees, doubts may just have been starting to fill the heads of Jock Stein's players

All that would change in the 63rd minute when John Clark found Bobby Murdoch in space deep in the Italians' half. The midfielder immediately switched the play to Jim Craig who had moved up from the right back position.

Craig waited before releasing the ball back across goal into a pocket of space. It was there that Tommy Gemmell appeared, screaming for a pass before torpedoing a drive beyond Sarti in goal.

Moments such as these were already an established part of his repertoire, but looking back on his historic goal Celtic's left back admitted things could have been very different. "As I came to shoot, a defender stopped and half turned his back on me. If he had taken another step it would have been very difficult for me to get the ball past him."

Having been comprehensively outplayed, Inter had nothing left to give, offering little resistance as their opponents continued to pound forward. Celtic scored a winner with just five minutes remaining and in the process became the first British team to win Europe's most prestigious club competition.

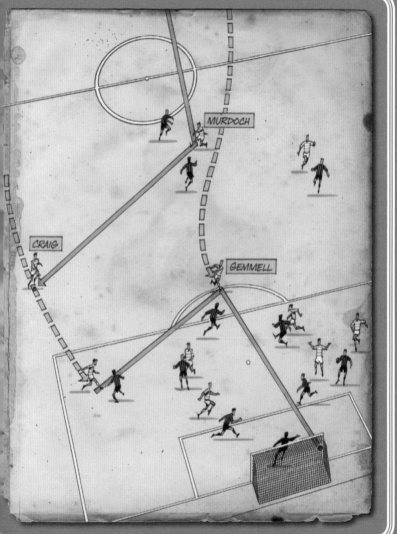

CRAIG

MURDOCH

GEMMELL

MAURICE JOHNSTON
1986 SCOTTISH PREMIER LEAGUE V ST MIRREN

Davie Hay's side had to win by three clear goals on the final day of the season to have any chance of stopping Hearts becoming champions.

On an unforgettable afternoon the Hoops went about their task in style, scoring five without reply. Their third, after 33 minutes, was the pick of the bunch.

It began when Danny McGrain flicked a ball over his head on the edge of his own box and exchanged passes with Murdo MacLeod. The veteran right back continued forward, moving the play to the feet of Paul McStay, who found Roy Aitken.

Aitken then returned the ball to McGrain, who slid it into Brian McClair's path. The breathtaking move was completed when the striker skipped around a Saints defender before laying it on for Maurice Johnston to tap in at the far post.

Some may have wiped this effort from their memories, since it was scored by a player who just three years later would be playing in the colours of Rangers. For others it has remained a thing of one-touch, non-stop beauty amid the mud and rain in Paisley.

The roar which greeted the goal was nothing compared to that at the end. Dundee had upset the odds, scoring twice in the second half and handing Celtic one of their most unexpected league titles.

JOHNSTON

McCLAIR

McGRAIN

AITKEN

McSTAY

McSTAY

McGRAIN

HENRIK LARSSON
2000 SCOTTISH PREMIER LEAGUE V RANGERS

It was the start of what was hoped would be a bright new dawn – Martin O'Neill had become manager after an utterly dismal nine months under John Barnes.

Celtic were leading 3-1 with 50 minutes played of O'Neill's first Old Firm match.

A goal kick from Jonathan Gould was met by Chris Sutton and cushioned into Henrik Larsson's path 40 yards out. Bursting forward the striker effortlessly shielded the bouncing ball from Rangers' midfielder Tugay, before showing just enough to tempt Konterman into a challenge. The big Dutchman's decision was to prove a bad one, as an instant later he was turned inside out by a nutmeg, leaving Larsson in a perfect position to finish with a deliciously angled chip over Klos in the Rangers goal.

Not only did this sensational effort put Celtic out of sight on the day, but it was one of the most accomplished goals in Larsson's long and celebrated career at the club; a piece of technical brilliance and artistry all too rarely seen in a traditionally helter-skelter derby fixture.

The eventual 6-2 destruction of Rangers would indeed set the tone for the next five years under O'Neill. In one match he seemed to have transformed both the players and the fans – instilling in each and every one of them the belief that they could once again dominate their old rivals.

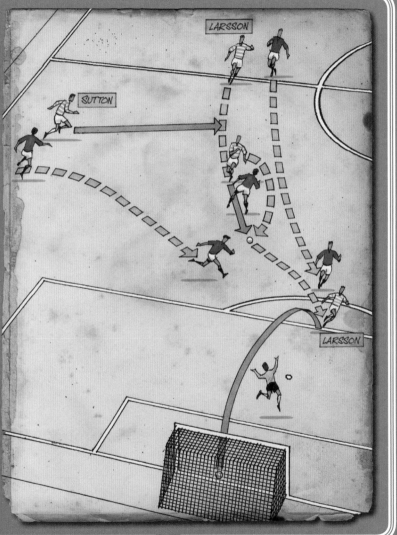

LARSSON

SUTTON

LARSSON

CHRIS SUTTON
2001 EUROPEAN CHAMPIONS LEAGUE V JUVENTUS

The Old Lady of Turin had come to Parkhead for what would prove to be the finest European tie there in many years. Even though they'd already qualified for the next round, Juventus still had the likes of Trezeguet, Del Piero and Nedved in their line-up. None would be a match, however, for Celtic's Slovakian magician Lubomir Movarcik. The 36-year-old had postponed retirement to have a crack at the Champions' League. Brought out of cold storage for very nearly his final big match encore, he proceeded to bamboozle Juve with all his great gifts.

Celtic could only pip Porto to second place in the group if they won and the Portuguese champions slipped up against Rosenborg. Inspired by Moravcik, the Bhoys swarmed all over their opponents.

Leading 3-2, with half an hour remaining, the moment came which confirmed the home side's dominance. A Moravcik free-kick was headed on by Bobo Balde; behind him, on the edge of the box, Chris Sutton had peeled away from his markers before expertly swivelling his body and lashing home the sweetest of volleys.

At the final whistle it emerged that a 4-3 win hadn't been enough to keep their hopes alive. Yet Sutton's strike would remain a treasured memory of the night when Celtic announced they were back in the big time.

SUTTON

JOHN HARTSON
2003 UEFA CUP V LIVERPOOL

Though Celtic had already knocked out Blackburn Rovers, few English observers truly believed they would be able to overcome Liverpool in the quarter-finals.

Needing to score after a 1-1 draw in Glasgow they set about their task with relish, having been reminded by Martin O'Neill that this was the perfect opportunity to "prove a point to England and Europe that you deserve respect, and that you are worthy of respect".

A goal from Alan Thompson just before half-time meant Celtic led on aggregate, but the tie would hang in the balance until the 82nd minute. It was then that John Hartson played a neat one-two with Henrik Larsson and shrugged off Jamie Carragher. With all his might, the chunky striker unleashed a never-to-be forgotten zinger which sent the Hoops into the last four of a European competition for the first time since 1974, and kept them on course for the final in Seville.

As an emotional Neil Lennon later said of the Welshman's exploits: "That was the best moment for me in the whole tournament, that goal. Just to see the big man wheel away to our fans, and looking at our bench and you know that you are 3-1 up at Anfield with ten minutes to go and there's just no way back for Liverpool."

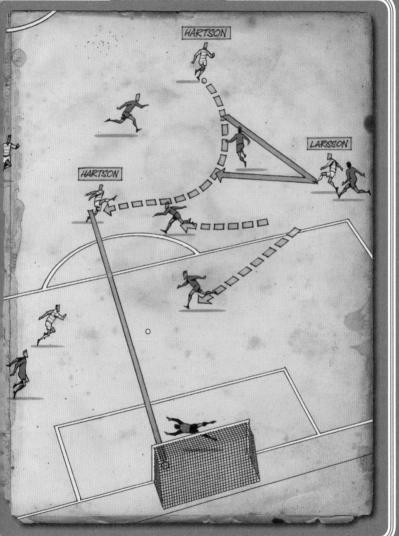

HARTSON

HARTSON

LARSSON

THE LISBON LIONS

There is a litany which every Celtic fan is expected to recite. It goes: Simpson, Craig and Gemmell, Murdoch, McNeill and Clark, Johnstone, Wallace, Chalmers, Auld and Lennox. These are the surnames of the first British team ever to win the European Cup.

They wrote themselves into the history books on 25th May 1967, having beaten Italian champions Inter Milan to the greatest prize in club football. Their collective endeavours and captivating style in the Portuguese capital brought them a special status; henceforth they would be known as The Lisbon Lions.

What has often been forgotten is that they did not play together that often. The first time they lined up as an XI was for a 4-0 win in January 1967, away to St Johnstone, and after that not until a scoreless draw with Aberdeen three months later.

They were bonded by a shared background, all being born within 30 miles of Celtic Park – something unimaginable today. With one exception, they'd all been on the books at Parkhead by the time Jock Stein returned in 1965 and many had been under his command in the reserves.

That was not the case with Ronnie Simpson, the
goalkeeper. Known as 'The Faither' he'd arrived from
Hibernian, aged 34, expecting to act as a back-up to
John Fallon. He prospered because of his coolness
under pressure, keeping clean sheets in half the games
he played for Celtic.

At left back Tommy Gemmell was a
bubbly character with a booming shot,
while Jim Craig on the right was steady
and orthodox, perhaps a reflection of his
university training as a dentist. It was a
background which, he admits, made him
stand out. "The other lads at Parkhead
wondered what I was going to be
like," he says. "Some of them definitely
thought I was going to speak Latin."

Billy McNeill, at centre half, had been
spotted as officer-class material from a
young age. As captain he possessed
great organisational qualities, was
excellent in the air and the tackle. His defensive
partner John Clark – playing just off McNeill as
sweeper – was a picture of vigilance, noted for his
superb reading of the game.

At right half was Bobby Murdoch, the man who
made the Lions tick. He'd take the ball straight from the
defence and land it, almost literally, on whichever blade of
grass he chose. Bertie Auld, a larger than life character,
was beside him in what was essentially a 4-2-4 formation.
He'd returned to Celtic early in 1965 after a spell with

Birmingham City having lost none of his swagger and confidence. Auld was the competitor supreme, a terrier with a deft touch.

Celtic's right wing belonged to the irrepressible Jimmy Johnstone. 'Jinky' had the ability to beat several players at a time through outrageous skill and guile. A born crowd pleaser, an opponent once said that playing against him was like "trying to pin a wave to the sand."

Bobby Lennox, on the opposite flank, was more straightforward, both in play and personality. The breathtaking pace he'd long honed on the beaches of his native Ayrshire was used to set up and score goals.

One of the main beneficiaries of the two wingers' efforts was Willie Wallace. He'd come to Celtic from Hearts in 1966, having been pinched from under Rangers' noses. He said he wouldn't have gone to Ibrox because he "could see the greater potential at Parkhead." Wallace was a highly-experienced forward, capable of shooting instantly with either foot. In the months leading up to the final he'd struck up a highly effective partnership with Steve Chalmers, the mainstay of the attack.

One of the veterans of the team, aged 30, Chalmers had come to professional football relatively late and was a well-established figure in the side even before 1965. Having been converted from inside forward, Chalmers was noted for his incredible stamina. Not only that, he was lethal in the box and totally unselfish.

These were the men destined to be held forever in

the limelight, but in the campaign which took them to Lisbon there were other heroes, such as John Hughes. 'Yogi' was awarded a European Cup winners' medal after playing in five of the games. Having regularly been part of the side in early May 1967, he picked up an injury which ruled him out of the final. It's something he's found hard to live with ever since. "It still stabs me in the heart when I think about it," he says.

High spirits at the celebration banquet in Lisbon after the match

He was not alone. Joe McBride, a striker bought from Motherwell in 1965, had bagged an incredible 36 goals before the Christmas holidays. Sadly for a dyed-in-the-wool supporter he picked up a knock against Aberdeen in late December which ruled him out for the next year.

The others who'd done their bit were Willie O'Neill and Charlie Gallacher. O'Neill had appeared four times in Europe at full back and Gallacher twice in midfield; his most notable moment being the corner which was headed home late in the second leg against Vojvodina, sending Celtic into the semis.

Billy McNeill, who scored that goal, hasn't forgotten these contributions. "Many people refer to the Lisbon Lions as the actual 11 who played that day," he says. "There were a lot more fine players involved in the all-round achievement… it was a genuine squad effort."

CELTIC COMIC STRIP HISTORY

2

CHEEKY CHARLIE TULLY WAS ONE OF THE MOST COLOURFUL CHARACTERS IN CELTIC'S HISTORY. HE ALSO POSSESSED SUBLIME FOOTBALLING SKILLS... IN A SCOTTISH CUP MATCH IN 1953...

WATCH THIS...

TAKING A CORNER-KICK, TULLY SENT THE BALL STRAIGHT INTO THE FALKIRK NET!

GOAL!

NO GOAL... TAKE THE CORNER AGAIN...

FOR SOME REASON THE REFEREE WASN'T HAPPY...

TULLY DID RETAKE IT... WITH PRECISELY THE SAME RESULT!

THIS TIME THE GOAL **WAS** ALLOWED TO STAND, AND HUNDREDS OF AMAZED AND DELIGHTED FANS STREAMED ON TO THE PITCH TO CONGRATULATE HIM!

IF YOU KNOW YOUR HISTORY
DELIGHT AND DESPAIR
1930-64

Having won the Scottish Cup in 1931 the victorious Celtic team took the trophy on a tour of North America where they were feted as the 'Irish holders of the World's Championship', with expats travelling hundreds of miles to see them play. Sadly, the celebratory mood would soon turn black.

John Thomson's tragic death from a skull fracture sustained during a game at Ibrox in September 1931 shocked everyone connected with the club, so much so that Willie Maley believed the loss of the young goalie "was responsible for many failures during the next few years".

Rangers continued to dominate throughout the early 1930s before a clutch of excellent youngsters – led by Jimmy Delaney and Malky MacDonald – emerged to assist Jimmy McGrory and others who were reaching the twilight of their careers.

Jimmy McMenemy returned as trainer and then, having gone 16 games with the loss of just a single point in 1936, the title was secured for the first time in a decade. The resurgence continued with a Scottish Cup triumph at the end of the next campaign; the Bhoys beating Aberdeen in front of a record 147,000 spectators.

There were further grounds for optimism with the club's 19th league championship and victory in the prestigious best-of-British Empire Exhibition trophy, both of which came during the club's golden jubilee in 1938. What the great and the good of football

didn't realise as they celebrated Celtic's half-century
with a lavish banquet was that it would be 16 years
before the league flag flew again over Parkhead.

Part of the reason for this was the laissez-faire
manner in which the directors reacted to the Second
World War. Normal football was suspended in
September 1939, before regional leagues were
formed to provide morale-boosting entertainment
for the masses.

Celtic keeper John
Thomson collides
with Rangers' Sam
English. He later died
from his injuries

Celtic's Bobby Evans tackles Sammy Cox of Rangers during a 1949 derby at Ibrox

While other clubs used the war-time travel restrictions to field top professionals – such as Stanley Matthews – who were stationed nearby, Celtic passed up the opportunity to re-strengthen by signing some of their past heroes. The club even ignored the pleas of Matt Busby who complained that he'd "waited almost three years" in the hope of playing at Parkhead.

Meanwhile, over at Ibrox, Rangers raked in a succession of cups and titles; in doing so creating an aura of invincibility around the club.

Out of 25 Old Firm encounters during the war Celtic won a paltry four, while the 1941 Glasgow Cup and the Charity Cup two years later were their only honours.

This drop in playing standards continued well into peacetime; the nadir being a scrambled 3-2 win over Dundee on the final day of the season in 1948 which avoided the calamity of relegation.

Celtic's new chairman – Robert Kelly – was stung into action, beefing up the team by signing Charlie Tully and Bobby Collins. They would both play their part in taking the Scottish Cup back to Paradise in 1951. Thankfully other men of character, notably Jock Stein and Neilly Mochan, were also arriving and would be on hand to power the side to their finest moment since the war: victory in the Coronation Cup.

This tournament was held in Glasgow in the spring of 1953 and again featured the eight leading British clubs of the day. Celtic had finished a woeful eighth in the league but were invited to compete primarily because they could be relied upon to draw vast crowds to the games.

It was something of a shock that they got as far as the final before overcoming a formidable Hibs side to again become unofficial champions of Britain – usurping this royalist celebration into the bargain. For that they had to thank Johnny Bonnar in goal. One newspaper described his second-half performance as "bordering on miraculous".

This was the spur for a magnificent run in 1953/54

which saw the Hoops race to their first league and
Scottish cup double since 1914. Frustratingly, it was
another false dawn as all the major honours escaped
over the next 12 months.

The inescapable truth was that while Celtic had
some brilliant individuals – men such as Tully and
Willie Fernie – as a team they were worryingly
inconsistent. Part of the problem was Robert Kelly's
autocratic style and tendency to order utterly bizarre
team selections. Without doubt, such interventions
contributed to needless cup final defeats in 1955
and 1956.

Despite these problems, the League Cup was
secured for the first time in the autumn of 1956 and
would be retained in the most thrilling and
unexpected manner 12 months later.

At the end of a sunny afternoon at Hampden,
Celtic goalkeeper Dick Beattie was left grinning in
delight as he held up seven extended fingers,
indicating to the ecstatic supporters that they really
weren't dreaming and had just witnessed a 7-1
destruction of Rangers which is still keenly
celebrated to this day in song.

Maddeningly, the lean years would continue
thereafter, with no major trophies being won for
the best part of another decade. The team which
humiliated Rangers began to break up almost
immediately after their finest hour-and-a-half: Sean
Fallon retired, Collins and Fernie were sold and Tully
returned to Ireland.

Celtic in 1955 with captain Jock Stein guarding the ball

After that, a rather unfair emphasis was placed on youth. Talented players were coming through – Billy McNeill and Bobby Murdoch among them – but their development was hindered as they were asked to fill the boots of experienced professionals. Still, the team was capable of playing entertaining football without being able to bridge the chasm which had emerged between the Old Firm.

Indeed, the fans were so upset by the 3-0 beating at Rangers' hands in the 1963 Cup final that thousands left long before the end, some even burning their scarves in protest. The Govan side had won the league

yet again, with Celtic finishing back in fourth. Things were no better the next season when all five derby matches were lost.

This situation left a depressed Neilly Mochan to conclude that "Celtic are finished", while the 25-year-old Billy McNeill admitted: "I was getting to the stage where I was ready for shifting." A saviour was required, and fast, if what seemed like a terminal decline was to be halted.

Celtic trounce Rangers 7-1 in the 1957 Scottish League Cup final

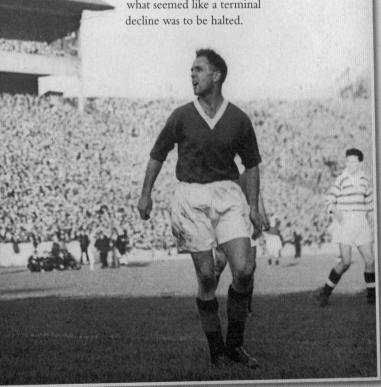

KIT PARADE

There are some football kits which are universally regarded as classics. Celtic's green and white hoops certainly fall into that category, being both instantly recognisable and much copied. The enduring popularity of the design has meant there have been few major alterations to the home shirt over the decades.

Celtic's original kit - the model of Victoriana

In fact, the outfit has become so strongly associated with the club that it may surprise some to learn that it was not always in use.

Rather, the first Celtic teams wore a white top with a green collar, long black shorts – or knickerbockers as they were called – and very probably thick woollen green-and-black-hooped socks. This all looks like pure Victoriana to the modern eye – the kind of thing suited only to men with elaborate moustaches.

In their second full season, 1889/90, a more distinctive pattern of vertical green and white stripes was used on the shirt. The socks turned to plain black, while some historians have intriguingly suggested that the shorts may have been a shade of blue – though much closer to that of Scotland than Rangers.

Then, as the football poet Daniel McDonagh wrote:

So in 1888 Celtic became a team,
But it was in 1903 that we saw the Hoops of green.

After more than a decade the stripes were rotated out of fashion and the hoops donned for the first time – against Partick Thistle that August.

Exactly why the change occurred is a mystery clouded by the passage of time, though it may have been an effort to make the players appear more physically imposing. White shorts were introduced at the same time and – tinkering with the socks aside – this would remain Celtic's standard uniform over the coming 60 years.

It was only when Jock Stein swept into Celtic Park as manager in 1965, with televised and European football growing in scale, that the wider viewing public began to familiarise themselves with what's still regarded today as the quintessential Celtic strip.

This featured the by-now traditional green and white bars on a round necked shirt. Players' numbers appeared on the shorts for the first time in 1960 and would be retained as another touch of understated elegance, along with plain white socks. As Stein himself said: "Celtic jerseys are not for second best, they don't shrink to fit inferior players."

If this sounded arrogant he had due cause, since the men he sent out to play in them were rarely anything other than winners.

The iconic hoops first appeared in 1903

The Lisbon Lions kit that made Celtic's strip recognisable around the world

For those not quite old enough to have the Lisbon Lions as their heroes, there was another Stein-inspired side — one sporting long hair and outsized sideburns — to worship in a remodelled version of the green and white. The new-fangled strip was worn from 1972 and featured a collar — reminiscent of the tops used from the mid-1930s through to the early 1960s — as well as a prominent V-shaped patch below the neck.

Towards the end of the decade the collar was removed again in favour of a straightforward V-neck.

At the same time the Celtic badge and that of the kit-makers, in this case Umbro, made it onto the jersey, where they have remained ever since. The material used also changed, from cotton to nylon.

However, the biggest alteration came in 1984 when Celtic took the plunge commercially, adding a shirt sponsor in an unusual joint venture with Rangers. The double glazing firm CR Smith paid £500,000 for an initial three year deal which, in fact, ran until 1991. The company explained that no sponsor "had dared to support one club for fear of alienating the fans of the other side".

A retro look was used to reflect the club's centenary in 1988. The jersey featured a granddad collar with a pop-button, and an updated version of the Celtic Cross badge, harking back to the original outfit. It was a huge hit with the fans.

In the early 1990s Ford controversially took over the sponsorship. The car manufacturer used their dealership brand – People's – in red text but refused to switch the colour of the Ford logo itself, meaning Celtic had

By 1988, a sponsor's name adorned the shirt worn by the likes of Paul McStay

You couldn't fail to notice Alan Stubbs in the 1996/97 away kit

to play with a blue smudge at the heart of their top.

When Scotland came fully into line with UEFA regulations on kits in 1994 Celtic's tradition of wearing numbers on their shorts was binned, albeit reluctantly.

The board had accepted, from the mid-1970s, that numerals had to be displayed on the back of shirts for European games, but always resisted this domestically. The new owner, Fergus McCann, considered paying a fine for every match in which the Bhoys refused to come into line. In the end, however, he thought better of it.

A succession of hoops of varying shapes and sizes came and went without fanfare during the 1990s, something which cannot be said for the fluorescent yellow and black away number which made its entrance in season 1996/97. In a decade of few bright spots this kit – worn by Paulo di Canio and Jorge Cadete – certainly caught the eye.

It also confirmed that the designers were hell bent

on using the change strip to demonstrate their full range of garish creativity. Unlikely as it seems, it was resurrected in the heavily marketed 'Bumble Bee' top of 2009/10.

An unprecedented episode concerned the home kit which was due to usher in the new Millennium. Umbro were forced to order a mass recall in 1999 when it emerged that a single cycle in the washing machine left it looking faded and bobbled.

Simple. Modern. Classic. The Hoops in 2007

Two years later there was uproar again when fans realised that large white panels had been inserted under the arms – effectively breaking the hoops. The anger melted away somewhat as the team won a domestic treble.

Umbro were dropped in 2005 after several decades, and replaced by Nike in a move described as the largest commercial contract Celtic had ever signed. While not everyone's idea of the perfect bedfellows, the American sports giant has consistently offered simple hooped designs which most supporters could feel at ease with.

**TERRACE
LEGENDS**

PATSY GALLACHER

There may never have been a more gifted player to wear the famous hoops. Those who were fortunate enough to have seen Patsy Gallacher in action regarded him as nothing less than a footballing genius.

When he arrived from Clydebank Juniors, the sight of this little Irishman did not immediately inspire confidence that greatness lay within his seemingly frail bones.

In fact, Jimmy Quinn was so concerned that he remarked, before Gallacher made his debut in 1911, that, "to put him on the park … would be manslaughter".

This was understandable. Gallacher had been born in a poor house in Donegal and remained painfully thin, with his jersey hanging from his body. Yet he would deal with the rigours of a tough professional game until he was almost 40 by displaying an enormous will to win and an absolute refusal to be physically intimidated.

Gallacher was essentially an enigma: he didn't look like a

footballer but, by the same token, he played the game like no one else could.

By 1912 he was already beginning to gather a reputation which would never leave him: as a dribbler extraordinaire, a forward of immense skill who sought to entertain, but never without purpose. He was always ready with the killer ball or a firecracker of a shot.

With very little moving footage, or even still pictures of his time in the game, it's hard to fully grasp just how good he was.

But these are the facts: in the years before and during the Great War Celtic were built around the player whose exploits and size brought him the affectionate nickname The Mighty Atom.

The Bhoys were so strong at this time that bookmakers would only offer odds with Celtic as the home side, even though they were playing away.

In his 15 years at Parkhead, six league titles, four Scottish Cups, four Glasgow Cups and 11 Charity Cups would be won.

The brilliant Rangers winger Alan Morton summed up Patsy Gallacher by paying this compliment: "There never was a player like him, I often wonder if we shall see his like again."

> ❝ **Patsy was the complete footballer. He had wonderful ball control, he had tricks of manipulation all his own** ❞
> Sir Robert Kelly

PATSY GALLACHER FACTFILE

Born: Ramelton, Ireland, 16th March 1891

Celtic appearances: 464

Celtic goals: 192

Honours won with Celtic:
Scottish League Championship (1914, 1915, 1916, 1917, 1919, 1922); Scottish Cup (1912, 1914, 1923, 1925)

Other clubs: Falkirk

International appearances:
Ireland, 12 caps; Irish Free State, 1 cap

JIMMY JOHNSTONE

The bare statistics of Jimmy Johnstone's career show he was a tremendous success, yet they fail to do justice to his devastating abilities with a football. Jinky was a dribbler sent to the east end of Glasgow by the Gods themselves.

At just 5ft 4in tall it seemed hardly credible that he could singlehandedly destroy defences, employing flawless balance to weave and spin past opponents in a non-stop swirl of wing play.

It was Celtic's great fortune that he was at his peak during Jock Stein's years in charge. Johnstone was central to the team which won nine championships in a row and Stein was the reason the player – an irrepressibly buoyant character with a wild streak – remained in the game for so long.

There are endless tales of his prowess, but none better than the time in 1968 when he destroyed Red Star Belgrade, scoring twice and setting up another three in a 5-1 win. Petrified of flying, Johnstone had been told that he wouldn't need to travel to Yugoslavia if Celtic were in command of the tie.

He also lit up Alfredo Di Stefano's testimonial against Real Madrid shortly after winning the European Cup. As he turned in a stellar performance 120,000 fans in the Bernabéu bellowed "Ole! " every time he touched the ball. Di Stefano himself said afterwards that the little winger had been among the best players he'd ever encountered.

ff On my first day as Scotland manager I had to call off practice after half an hour, because nobody could get the ball off wee Jimmy Johnstone JJ
Tommy Docherty

Johnstone summed up Celtic's style as being "like the Dutch speeded-up". Rightly, over the years the tributes would flow – he was 'The Flying Flea', and the 'Lord of the Wing'. Films were made to highlight his talents and a Fabergé Egg was designed in his honour, the first made since the Tsars ruled Russia. A statue of him in full-flight now adorns the front of the ground – a lasting monument to his magic.

In 2002 he was voted Celtic's Greatest Ever Player. The award came a year after he was diagnosed with Motor Neurone disease, the condition which sadly took his life in early 2006.

Born: 30th September 1944, Uddingston

Celtic appearances: 515

Celtic goals: 130

Honours won with Celtic: Scottish League Championship (1967 1968, 1969, 1970, 1971, 1972, 1973, 1974); Scottish Cup (1967 1971, 1972, 1974); Scottish League Cup (1966, 1967, 1970, 1975); European Cup (1967)

Other clubs: Sheffield United, Dundee, Elgin City, Shelbourne, San Jose Earthquakes

International appearances: Scotland, 23 caps

JIMMY JOHNSTONE FACTFILE

HENRIK LARSSON

It was strange that the King of Kings didn't arrive in a blaze of glory. Perhaps it was the price tag, a mere £650,000, or maybe it was a tepid debut in which he passed straight to Chic Charnley who promptly scored the winner for Hibs.

There was the distant recollection of a dreadlocked youngster who'd dazzled for Sweden at the World Cup in 1994 and then sunk without trace. Three years later he'd touched down in Glasgow and with a shrug told reporters that he'd "been long enough in Holland, Celtic looks like a very good club".

Under his old mentor, Wim Jansen, he was transformed again into a shining jewel of an attacker, putting an unhappy time with Feyenoord behind him by spearheading Celtic's drive to halt Rangers winning ten league titles in a row.

The Bhoys would be champions again and though Jansen quickly departed, Henrik stayed – despite an offer from Sir Alex Ferguson. The cult of Larsson was born.

First he confounded the experts by returning, months

ahead of schedule, from a horrific leg break sustained in the autumn of 1999. His timing was impeccable. A new era was beginning and Larsson's unstoppable, sparkling brilliance allied to Martin O'Neill's considerable managerial abilities meant it would be glorious.

> **❝ Henrik is a magician. We need a few better words in the English language than 'fantastic' and 'marvellous' to describe him ❞**
> Martin O'Neill

The 2000/01 season had many highs: the 6-2 'demolition derby' against Rangers and the first domestic treble for 30 years. Larsson was also crowned Europe's top striker, taking the Golden Boot with an astounding 53 goals.

By now the dreadlocks were shorn, but his haul of domestic honours would continue to grow. In Europe he provided some memorable Champions League displays and was instrumental in the club's run to the UEFA Cup final of 2003 – scoring two memorable goals in the final against Porto.

"It's been so special for me to play here" he said with tears on his cheeks after his last match in 2004. He then left for two highly successful "fun" periods with Barcelona and Manchester United, having sealed his place among the giants of the Celtic story.

Born: 20th September 1971, Helsingborg, Sweden
Celtic appearances: 315
Celtic goals: 242
Honours won with Celtic:
Scottish League Championship (1998, 2001, 2002, 2004); Scottish Cup (2001, 2004); Scottish League Cup (1998, 2001); UEFA Cup Runners-Up (2003)

Other clubs: Helsingborgs, Feyenoord, Barcelona
International appearances: Sweden, 106 caps

HENRIK LARSSON FACTFILE

DANNY MCGRAIN

Few players have served Celtic for so long and with as much distinction. During the course of 20 years with the club Danny McGrain would become a greatly admired and truly world class defender.

It could all have been so different. He'd grown up as a Rangers fan and been desperate to play for them. However, one of their scouts assumed that Daniel Fergus McGrain could only be of Catholic stock. He was wrong, and Celtic – a club which has only ever cared about ability – stepped in.

Arriving in the glorious month of May 1967, McGrain joined the Quality Street gang of players which included Kenny Dalglish and Davie Hay. Here was a group so blessed with talent they would shortly be pushing the Lisbon Lions for places in the first team.

McGrain – with his distinctive black beard – would make his name as a swashbuckling and tenacious warrior of a right back. He was, as Billy McNeill remarked, "a real cruel tackler at times". He could also play left back and even centre half if required.

Yet it was his indomitable spirit in adversity which helped set him apart. Neither a fractured skull nor being diagnosed with diabetes stood in his way.

He also spent more than a year on the sidelines with a niggling ankle injury, something which caused him to sit out the 1978 World Cup in Argentina. Scotland missed him terribly – proving Rod Stewart right when he sang: "I only wish we had Danny McGrain."

He was appointed Celtic captain in 1977, a position he would hold for the next decade. Along the way McGrain would more than play his part in highs such as the league-deciding triumph over Rangers in 1979, the Cup Final comeback of 1985 and the destruction of St Mirren a year later which pipped Hearts to the title.

Danny's dedication has continued through his work as a reserve team coach at Parkhead – where he is still viewed by many as the best full back ever to have worn the hooped jersey.

> ** Nobody replaces Danny, you have to understand that you are following an absolute legend. He was just unbelievable **
>
> Chris Morris

DANNY McGRAIN FACTFILE

Born: 1st May 1950, Glasgow
Celtic appearances: 663
Celtic goals: 7
Honours won with Celtic:
Scottish League Championship (1973, 1974, 1977, 1979, 1981, 1982, 1986); Scottish Cup (1974, 1975, 1977, 1980, 1985); Scottish League Cup (1975, 1983)

Other clubs: Hamilton Academical

International appearances: Scotland, 62 caps

JIMMY MCGRORY

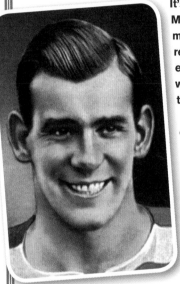

It's highly doubtful that Jimmy McGrory's achievements will ever be matched. Strikers build their reputations on goals and that explains why for many he is still worshipped as the greatest Celt of them all.

Having made his debut at the start of January 1923, the forward from the tough Glasgow Irish enclave of the Garngad would go on to have another half century of official involvement with the club, eventually rising to the post of manager.

Yet this most decent of men, the son of a gasworks labourer, will always be remembered primarily for his on-field heroics. He came to be known as the 'Human Torpedo' and 'Mermaid' for an uncanny heading prowess, with one goalkeeper having three fingers smashed trying to save a rocket from the striker's forehead.

On three occasions in 1926/27 McGrory scored five times in one game, and on another three he netted four, setting a new record of 49 goals in a season. The following year he achieved a new world record of eight goals in a single match.

By the time he retired in 1937, his total would reach a mind-boggling 550 strikes, a figure which still stands as the highest in British football. That astonishing scoring record also includes 410 strikes in 408 league games.

Strange then, that he won so few international honours, turning out for Scotland only a handful of times.

He did, however, notch a memorable late winner in a game against England in Glasgow in 1933, a moment which led to wild celebrations in the ground and produced what was referred to, for the first time, as The Hampden Roar.

As ridiculous as it seems, in 1928 Celtic actually tried to sell their prized asset. While travelling via London on pilgrimage to Lourdes, McGrory was twice asked by the legendary Herbert Chapman to sign for Arsenal. He refused, even after being offered a blank cheque with which to set his own signing-on fee.

The thrill of playing for the club he truly loved was all he wished for in football. As the player himself once put it: "McGrory of Arsenal just never sounded as good as McGrory of Celtic."

ff He did more than score goals; he converted countless numbers to the belief that football was all there was worth living for JJ
Archie Macpherson

Born: 26th April 1904, Glasgow

Celtic appearances: 472

Celtic goals: 529

Honours won with Celtic: Scottish League Championship (1926, 1936); Scottish Cup (1925, 1931, 1933, 1937)

Other clubs: Clydebank (loan)

International appearances: Scotland, 7 caps

JIMMY MCGRORY FACTFILE

BILLY MCNEILL

CUT ALONG HERE

A TY-PHOO SERIES OF 24

Billy McNeill (signature)

No. 18 BILLY McNEILL

INTERNATIONAL FOOTBALL STARS

BILLY McNEILL
(Celtic and Scotland)

Signed by Celtic in 1958, Billy McNeill quickly made his mark. Captain of this club, he has also led his country. He scored the winning goal in the 1965 Scottish Cup Final and in 1966 Celtic topped the Scottish League. His collection of caps includes 17 full International and 7 'Under 23s'. He also has 10 Scottish League medals.

The sight of an imperious Billy McNeill, with the European Cup raised above his head in Lisbon, is one of the most enduring images in football.

The captain of the first British side to become champions of the continent, back in 1967, would qualify as a legend for that feat alone.

This strapping blond of Lithuanian descent had come to Parkhead from Blantyre Victoria in 1957. Having made his debut aged 18, his career stalled until Jock Stein returned as manager in 1965. McNeill then started the club's golden era by scoring a memorable headed winner in that season's Scottish Cup final.

By the time he retired a decade later, McNeill would have 23 winners' medals to show for his considerable efforts as an imposing defender who was both commanding in the air and tidy on the ground. He was, in short, Celtic's rock.

McNeill has long been

regarded as a gentleman, someone who always has time for the supporters and is capable of diplomacy even in the face of extreme provocation. After the notorious debacle of the World Club Championship, against a violent and unsporting Racing Club of Argentina, an opponent who feared he was about to be assaulted was astonished to be offered a handshake and an exchange of shirts instead.

❝ One of the greatest Celts of all time, an inspiring captain and a model for every young footballer ❞
Jock Stein

Even his nickname hints at greatness. He'd come to be known as Cesar after Cesar Romero, the actor who played the getaway driver in the original *Ocean's Eleven* film; McNeill being the only Celtic player who had a car at the time. Yet post-Lisbon this morphed into Caesar, in homage to the great Roman general.

After being carried aloft from the Hampden turf having played his last match in 1975, McNeill's heart remained with what he described as a club "founded for the right reasons". He would return twice as manager, and in 2009 he became Celtic's official ambassador. But as a poll of fans demonstrated a few years ago, he will always be regarded primarily as The Hoops' greatest ever captain.

Born: 2nd March 1940, Bellshill, Lanarkshire
Celtic appearances: 813
Celtic goals: 38
Honours won with Celtic:
Scottish League Championship (1966, 1967 1968, 1969, 1970, 1971, 1972, 1973, 1974);
Scottish Cup (1965, 1967 1969, 1971, 1972, 1974, 1975);
Scottish League Cup (1966, 1967 1968, 1969, 1970, 1975);
European Cup (1967)
Other clubs: None
International appearances: Scotland, 29 caps

BILLY MCNEILL FACTFILE

PAUL MCSTAY

If ever there was a player with Celtic in his blood it was Paul McStay. His two great uncles had played for the club and one had later been manager. Repeating history, McStay's own elder bother – Willie – would break into the team alongside him.

Yet it was Paul, with barnstorming appearances for Scotland's youth sides, who was the one tipped for the top. His talent was such that he was thrust into the limelight, aged just 17, in January 1982, scoring on his league debut against Aberdeen.

He would quickly earn the tag Maestro for his sumptuous technique, the hallmark of which was an uncanny ability to beat opponents with devilishly quick feet, before delivering an exquisite pass.

Throughout the 1980s his reputation grew to the point when this shy young man came to be regarded as the finest player of his generation in Scotland. In the centenary season of 1987/88 McStay was at his peak, regularly turning in untouchable displays which would secure the league and Scottish Cup double.

His superb volley and all-round showing in the New Year victory at Ibrox prompted the Glasgow Herald to declare: "His was a performance to match the balance and grace of Nureyev, the gentle arrogance of Beckenbauer and the chilling accuracy of a hired assassin."

In the years which followed McStay would be one of very few bright lights at Parkhead, effectively carrying the team as Rangers dominated.

He had the chance to depart for Italy, England and France – environments where he would have thrived, as was proved by his outstanding play for Scotland at Euro 92. In the end he explained he'd only wanted to be "Paul McStay of Celtic".

A persistent ankle injury forced his early retirement in 1997. Before that came the heartbreaking penalty miss which handed the League Cup to Raith Rovers. But ultimately there was the glorious swansong of the 1995 Scottish Cup win against Airdrie, in which a delighted McStay captained his beloved Celtic to their first trophy in six years.

> **He was one hell of a player, a gentleman and a true Celt who gave everything for the club. Luckily for him he had outstanding ability**
> Billy Stark

Born: 22nd October 1964, Hamilton

Celtic appearances: 677

Celtic goals: 72

Honours won with Celtic: Scottish League Championship (1982, 1986, 1988); Scottish Cup (1985, 1988, 1989, 1995); Scottish League Cup (1983)

Other clubs: None

International appearances: Scotland, 76 caps

PAUL MCSTAY FACTFILE

JIMMY QUINN

The story of Jimmy Quinn has a romantic hue which few footballers today can match. He was the original cult hero of Parkhead.

Having already spurned the advances of Sunderland – which was one of the biggest clubs in England at the time – it had taken serious persuasion to get him to turn out for Celtic. This shy, pipe-smoking coal miner was perfectly content to keep playing junior football in Lanarkshire, apparently unsure of his chances in the senior game.

Quinn scored when he made his debut in the early days of 1901 and he also lit up that season's Cup Final with a goal, having beaten six Hearts players.

However, he would be played on the right and, more often, the left wing until the middle of the following year. After being urged by a director to sell the player, Willie Maley moved him to centre forward.

It was a masterstroke which would soon make Quinn

the most feared attacker in Britain.

As a striker he was almost faultless. He was a nippy bundle of bravery with a cannonball shot, a result of the enormous strength his days in the mines had given him. Quinn was tough too, and had to be at just 5ft 8in, once remarking: "I used to play with the blood running down my boots."

He would seal his reputation in the Scottish Cup final of 1904. Rangers had stormed into an early 2-0 lead but The Mighty Quinn drew Celtic level with two fizzing shots before half time.

Then, as he explained, with ten minutes remaining he "dashed right through the Rangers' defence and finished with a real trimmer which brought us our first Scottish Cup badges and the confidence which made our team for the next six years". It was the first hat-trick scored by a Celtic player against Rangers in a major competition.

Quinn was central to a side which won the league every season from 1905 to 1910 and remained a scourge of goalkeepers until forced to retire with knee trouble in 1915. He is still the fifth highest goal-scorer in the club's history.

> ❝ **The keystone in the greatest team Celtic ever had** ❞
>
> Willie Maley

JIMMY QUINN FACTFILE

Born: Croy, Lanarkshire, 8th July 1878

Celtic appearances: 311

Celtic goals: 217

Honours won with Celtic: Scottish League Championship (1905, 1906, 1907, 1908, 1909, 1910); Scottish Cup (1904, 1907, 1908, 1911, 1912)

Other clubs: None

International appearances: Scotland, 11 caps

JOHN THOMSON

Known as The Prince of Goalkeepers, John Thomson's untimely death and his uncanny ability between the sticks have assured him a rightful and lasting place among the most eminent Celts.

Signed at the age of 17, and rescued – like many others of that era – from a life in the pits, the Fifer was instantly recognised as an athlete of supreme agility and considerable bravery. Asked why he took so many risks by diving headlong at opponents' feet he said: "I'm a goalkeeper and it's my job to never take my eyes off the ball."

Aged just 22 and already Scotland's goalie, it looked as though fame and honours were to be the currency of his years in the game. Sadly, it was not to be.

In a match against Rangers at Ibrox in 1931, he once again demonstrated his fearless nature by throwing himself towards the onrushing Rangers' striker, Sam English.

The clash left Thomson frozen on the turf, as English, who was utterly blameless, limped away. The goalkeeper had suffered a depressed fracture of the skull and despite frantic efforts to save his life, he died later that evening.

News of his passing was a terrible shock to Scottish society. Twenty thousand people saw his coffin leave Glasgow and another 50,000 attended the funeral in his native village of Cardenden.

Perhaps the best of the many tributes to be paid came from the sports broadcaster and poet, John Arlott, who wrote: "He was a great player who came to the game as a boy and left it as a boy. He had no predecessor, no successor. He was unique."

John Thomson will never be forgotten as long as there are Celtic supporters. Songs and books have been written in his honour, and he now has a permanent place in the SFA's Hall of Fame.

More than that, there is still a steady stream of visitors who make the pilgrimage each year to his graveside in a quiet corner of a west Fife cemetery.

> **He had the ability of a ballet dancer to jump much higher than other people. There was a great deal of magic about what he was doing**
>
> Desmond White

Born: 28th January 1909

Celtic appearances: 188

Honours won with Celtic: Scottish Cup (1927, 1931)

Other clubs: None

International appearances: Scotland, 4 caps

JOHN THOMSON FACTFILE

CHARLIE TULLY

Tully was nothing less than a superstar, a crowd-puller without equal in the history of the Scottish game. His immense skill and roguish personality meant he was tailor-made for Celtic.

He was instantly lionised by the support. A new hero was badly needed after the team had escaped relegation by the skin of their teeth.

Coming over the water from Belfast Celtic in 1948 as an inside left, Tully would spend the next decade teasing and tricking defences, with a twinkle in his eye.

His party piece was waving his arms at the spot where he was about to deliver the ball, before suddenly going away on a meandering run instead. Supporters also roared their approval when he scored directly from a corner or bounced the ball off defenders' heads at throw-ins.

The match which made him the darling of Parkhead was

a 3-1 Old Firm victory in the League Cup soon after his debut. Tully made a mockery of Rangers' Iron Curtain defence, dancing around them as he pleased. A week later he would be instrumental again, as Celtic won their first trophy since the war – beating Third Lanark to take the Glasgow Cup.

ff He was a genius, he was so bright at the game and just so intelligent JJ
Pat Crerand

Soon his fame prompted Tully ties, Tully cocktails and even green Tully ice cream. The joke in Glasgow at the time was that the Pope was visiting the city and the player was showing him around. People were saying to each other: 'Who's that with Charlie Tully?'

He and the rest of the team were actually on their way to the Vatican in 1950 when, sailing to Brussels, Tully spotted Bing Crosby and joined him for a drink, before getting the popular American singer to give the squad his rendition of *I Belong to Glasgow*.

Cheek and charm were always his companions. Once, before a game against England, he asked Alf Ramsey if he enjoyed playing for his country. "I do Mr Tully", came the response, to which he replied "make the most of it today, it might be the last chance you get."

Born: 11th July 1924, Belfast
Celtic appearances: 319
Celtic goals: 47
Honours won with Celtic:
Scottish League Championship (1954); Scottish Cup (1951, 1954); Scottish League Cup (1957, 1958); Coronation Cup (1953)
Other clubs: Belfast Celtic, Cork Hibernians, Stirling Albion
International appearances: Northern Ireland, 10 caps

CHARLIE TULLY FACTFILE

OLD FIRM

The phrase Old Firm which has for so long described the world's most famous derby does not stretch all the way back to the opening salvos involving the sides. In fact when Celtic first took on Rangers in May 1888, relations were cordial.

After Celtic's victory in that original encounter both teams repaired to St Mary's Hall for refreshments and an evening which was said to have been of "the happiest character". This bonhomie continued with joint social evenings and invitations to watch each other take on English opposition in the years thereafter. One newspaper even reported that "the light blues are favourites with the Parkhead crowd."

Transformation into a serious cross-city rivalry also stemmed in part from this mutual cooperation; the clubs stood shoulder to shoulder in arguing for professionalism. In doing so they effectively killed off Queen's Park, the amateurs who'd dominated the early years of the game.

Celtic replaced 'The Spiders' as the main force in the land, sweeping away all opponents, Rangers included. In fact it was not until 1893 that the Ibrox club managed a victory in the fixture. After that the Rangers' support began to increase and they slowly came to be seen as the team best placed to answer calls for a home-grown tartan challenge to Celtic's pre-eminence. Ibrox would become a Mecca for what the *Glasgow Observer* described as "the anti-Celt".

It was during these closing years of the 19th century that

the Old Firm tag was first used. It stuck because the sides were competing against each other regularly for the major honours and accruing vast sums of money in gate receipts. In 1894 Celtic had an annual return of £10,142 – a British record for the time. The Old Firm were becoming big business and together, in the two decades after 1899, they won more than 30 major trophies.

From then on the antipathy would grow. This was in part thanks to an influx of hard-line Protestant shipbuilders from Northern Ireland and changes at the top of Rangers in 1912, both of which seemed to harden attitudes towards Catholics. Years later, looking back on this era, Willie Maley strongly believed it to have been the point when Rangers' ethos was defined by religion.

An officer checks his watch at the start of a 1949 derby at Ibrox

This no-Catholic policy continued throughout the managerial reign of Bill Struth (from 1920) and beyond, while by contrast Celtic fielded several stars who were not necessarily natural followers of The Hoops. This inclusive outlook was reinforced when Jock Stein – a Protestant – took over as manager.

Needless to say, regardless of the decade or the political climate Old Firm matches have always been capable of producing volcanic eruptions. These go back at least as far as the riot at the Scottish Cup final of 1909. In May 1940, as Catholics and Protestants from Scotland fought on the same side in Europe, there were clashes at Ibrox.

The violence would continue throughout that decade with the terrifying phenomenon known as 'Bottle Parties'. 'Rex' – the correspondent of the *Sunday Mail* – reported in 1949 that "a shower of bottles emerged from the crowd, raining down on the field, track and just as often, fellow-supporters".

These incidents were not always related to excess alcohol, but also to events on the pitch. This was the case with an infamous clash between Charlie Tully and Sammy Cox in the late 1940s, Tully being kicked by the Rangers' full back in what was described, subtley, as "the groin".

McAvennie, Woods and Butcher square up during the infamous 1987 derby at Ibrox

By far the worst incident came almost 40 years later after Celtic won the Scottish Cup at Hampden, having beaten Rangers 1-0 in 1980. Inexplicably, Strathclyde Police had decided to concentrate their resources outside Hampden.

This was a blunder which led to a riot when the players had gone to celebrate with the green and white legions behind the goal at their traditional end of the ground. Millions watched live on TV as mounted police charged hundreds of supporters who were scrapping on the pitch. Over 100 people were injured, with 50 requiring hospital treatment.

These events prompted changes in the law which, among other things, banned booze from stadiums in Scotland. But even these measures failed to take the sting out of a fixture which is still capable of boiling over into outright ugliness.

It may seem strange then that the players, in most eras, have remained on friendly terms. They would often build up personal relationships through their time away with Scotland, as well as moving in the same social circles in Glasgow.

As for the fans, while never seeing eye-to-eye over football, they do tend to live and work side by side without any significant problems. In fact at times of great trauma there have been laudable cessations in hostilities: the passing of Celtic greats John Thomson and Tommy Burns showed this to be the case, as did the horrific Ibrox disasters of 1902 and 1971, which touched so many families.

Though most observers tend to feel that it is nigh-on impossible to separate the two sides, it should be pointed out that Celtic's fan base is becoming increasingly uneasy about the use of the phrase Old Firm. They feel it suggests that the clubs are merely two sides of the same coin, sharing similar problems.

They argue that this is grossly unfair as there has never been a policy based on religion at Parkhead. During the early part of this century supporters groups even took steps to highlight their objections both to sectarianism and racism, while calling for ties to be cut with Rangers when it comes to shared shirt sponsorship. One large banner at Parkhead perhaps summed this up best by stating: 'Old Firm… It's Time to Walk Alone… No More Guilt by Association'.

IF YOU KNOW YOUR HISTORY
THE GRANDEST TEAM
1965-78

Some men prove unable of living up to their reputations – not so Jock Stein. Returning to Parkhead in March 1965 dubbed The Miracle Man, the new manager grabbed a club with dwindling status by the throat and forced it to the very top of the world game in less than two years.

In that short time every domestic honour was secured, including two championships and, most thrillingly of all, the European Cup in 1967. Inter Milan, the architects of ultra-defensive football, were swept aside in the heat of Lisbon. The final score was 2-1 but Celtic were a tour de force of what Stein called "pure beautiful football." In fact his squad had been exactly that throughout a season in which they swept the boards, winning every competition that they entered.

Strangely they hardly got to defend their European crown, being eliminated in the first round against Dynamo Kiev next time around. That was merely the entrée to the bitter main course of international competition which was about to be served.

The World Club Championship play-off saw Racing Club of Argentina beaten 1-0 in the autumn of 1967. The return leg in Buenos Aires was less a football match than an advert for outright thuggery. Celtic were attacked and spat on. As Billy McNeill recalls: "The reception we got at the game was nothing short of horrific."

Racing won 2-1 to level the aggregate score and a

deciding match, in Montevideo, turned into another brutal farce. The Argentinians punched, kicked and provoked their way to a 1-0 victory in which four Scots were sent off, plus another two from the home side.

Billy McNeill lines up before the 1967 European Cup final

Thankfully the bitter experience in South America failed to knock Celtic out of their splendid stride at

Disgraceful scenes marred the 1967 World Club Championship play-off in Montevideo

home. With the League Cup already won the championship itself was secured for the third consecutive year.

The pattern of success was repeated, and bettered, in 1968/69 with a domestic treble, though the European Cup remained a disappointment – by the exceptional standards of those times – with AC Milan squeezing through a tight quarter-final encounter.

After that several players, Joe McBride and Willie O'Neill included, were allowed to depart. They were replaced by a clutch of home grown youngsters who'd help continue to bring success, with another title and League Cup triumph bagged by the time the Bhoys reached their second European Cup final, in 1970.

Having humbled Leeds United home and away in an epic 'Battle of Britain' semi-final Celtic went down 2-1 to Feyenoord. It was Lisbon in reverse, this time they were the favourites and the Dutch outfit were catastrophically underestimated.

The defeat was "the low point in our careers," according to Bobby Lennox. They would be viewed as one of the very best teams around for a long time to come, but this was a lost chance to place Celtic forever among the continental elite.

They comfortably managed to stay on top in their own backyard though, bouncing back to defeat Rangers in the final of the Scottish Cup and take a sixth title in succession the following season. This was a considerable landmark since it equalled the achievement of the great Hoops' side back in the first years of the century.

Celtic won the first of a two-legged affair 1-0

That record was broken in 1971/72 with another double – culminating in a stunning 6-1 Scottish Cup final defeat of Hibs. There was also a fourth European Cup semi in seven seasons, but this time

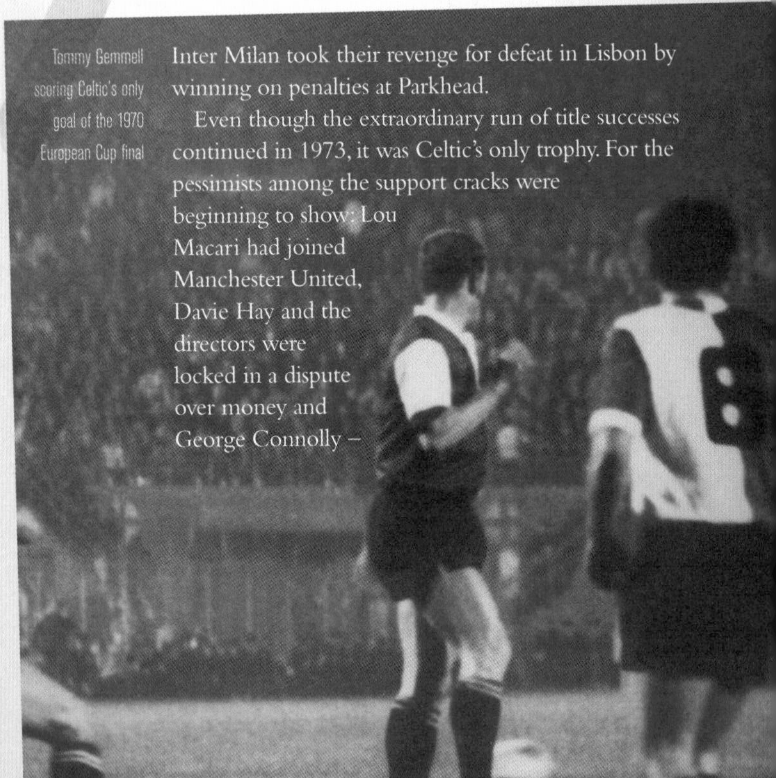

Tommy Gemmell
scoring Celtic's only
goal of the 1970
European Cup final

Inter Milan took their revenge for defeat in Lisbon by winning on penalties at Parkhead.

Even though the extraordinary run of title successes continued in 1973, it was Celtic's only trophy. For the pessimists among the support cracks were beginning to show: Lou Macari had joined Manchester United, Davie Hay and the directors were locked in a dispute over money and George Connolly –

a sublimely gifted but deeply unhappy sweeper/ midfielder – was soon to walk away from the game forever.

Not even these mounting personnel problems and another scrape with cynical continental tactics, at the hands of Atletico Madrid in 1974, could stand in the way of a world-record ninth successive league championship and the fifth double under Stein.

Kenny Dalglish heads past Gary Sprake in a 1973 testimonial for Jack Charlton against Leeds at Elland Road

It was a magnificent sequence brought to an end 12 months later when, having taken both domestic cups, Rangers ended Celtic's dreams of a treble and a tenth straight title. On top of that Billy McNeill retired, aged 35. Far more serious was the news that Stein himself had been very badly hurt in an accident on a notorious stretch of road in southern Scotland.

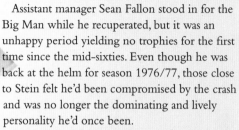

Assistant manager Sean Fallon stood in for the Big Man while he recuperated, but it was an unhappy period yielding no trophies for the first time since the mid-sixties. Even though he was back at the helm for season 1976/77, those close to Stein felt he'd been compromised by the crash and was no longer the dominating and lively personality he'd once been.

With both the championship and the Scottish Cup regained at Rangers' expense in May 1977, the good habits of the past dozen years seemed to have returned. It was not the case; decay had set in and Kenny Dalglish would take his world-class talents to Liverpool before the summer was out.

This was the prelude to Stein's own departure. His last year in charge, 1977/78, was clouded by injury to key players and questions about those brought in to replace Dalglish. The final table showed the Hoops in a poor fifth spot and behind the scenes the board had already taken the painful decision to look for a new boss.

Stein knew it was coming, but for a man who was said to have 'slept with his eyes open, thinking about football', stepping aside – in May 1978 – was hard to take. His successor, Billy McNeill, was the only person capable of taking the mantle from a true giant of the game; one who'd won an astonishing 25 trophies over 13 years and made himself – as Bill Shankly rightly put it – "immortal".

CELTIC COMIC STRIP HISTORY

3

1970...AND JOCK STEIN'S CELTIC WERE IN LEEDS FOR THE FIRST LEG OF THEIR EUROPEAN CUP CLASH...

SORRY... BUT LEEDS ARE WEARING WHITE SOCKS, **YOU** MUST CHANGE...

BUT THESE ARE ALL WE HAVE...

LEEDS' BOSS DON REVIE, WELL KNOWN FOR HIS MIND GAMES, OFFERED TO HELP...

WE CAN LEND YOU THESE...

...OR THESE!

BUT THEY ARE BOTH **RANGERS** COLOURS...

WE'LL WEAR THE **RED** ONES...

JOCK STEIN REASONED: 'THEY'LL LOOK ORANGE UNDER THE FLOODLIGHTS. OUR FANS WILL THINK WE'RE PLAYING IN THE COLOURS OF THE IRISH FLAG... THEY'LL LIKE THAT!'

THEY DID! CELTIC WON AN EPIC TIE, AND WENT ON TO MEET FEYENOORD IN THE FINAL...

TACTICS

MALEY PATENTS THE CELTIC STYLE

Celtic are known for playing the game in an attractive and dynamic way. This was institutionalised when Willie Maley hung up his boots to become manager. By 1904 he was developing a team which would win six championships in a row, sealing Celtic's reputation as football purists. The 04 vintage were truly a blend of youth and experience which managed to get the best out of several outstanding individual talents.

At full back, in front of Davie Adams in goal, was the veteran Willie Orr, a supremely consistent performer. He was partnered in the classic 2-3-5 combination of the times by the small but lightening fast Donald McLeod.

The half back line was one of the greatest in the club's history. Willie Loney, a brick wall of a centre half, tackled as if his life depended on it. On either side of him there was 'Sunny' Jim Young, noted for his brilliance in the air, and captain Jimmy Hay – an excellent reader of the game who could quickly sense how best to snuff out threatening moves.

These were the men who allowed the forward quintet to flourish. The tricky Alec Bennett was stationed on the right wing and had the considerable benefit of Jimmy McMenemy, one of the game's great playmakers, to his left.

Peter Somers was another magician at inside left from where he was able to feed 'The Dancer' – Davie Hamilton – as he sped down the left wing to deliver prefect crosses. Capitalising on these riches was the indomitable Jimmy Quinn at centre forward, strong, direct and always willing to bring others into the attack.

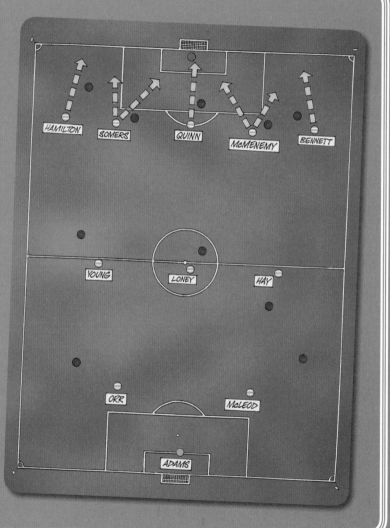

STEIN'S MAGICAL MOVES

Said to have been "miles ahead" of other coaches, even early in his managerial career, it's thought Jock Stein's interest in the tactical side of the game came from watching the peerless Hungarian 'Magical Magyars' of Puskas et al destroy England 6-3 at Wembley. The future Celtic manager looked on from the stands that day in 1953 and drank in this singular lesson of how football should be played.

Most obviously that was transferred into the thrilling attacking character of his teams. Positional tinkering was required to achieve this: first Bobby Murdoch was moved back from the forward line to a berth in midfield where his passing skills could best be utilised. After that Bertie Auld, who'd been an orthodox winger, was converted into an inside forward, giving balance to the side.

The manager relied on mobility in the wide areas where the full backs, Tommy Gemmell and Jim Craig, were expected to overlap. He also made sure his team mixed it physically, demonstrating they weren't prepared to be intimidated.

Perhaps the most innovative manoeuvre concerned corners. In his first few matches in charge – leading up to the Scottish Cup final of 1965 – Stein had encouraged Billy McNeill to sprint into the box for these set-pieces. What seems obvious to us today was tactical dynamite at the time.

With eight minutes to go in the final the scores were tied at 2-2. Bobby Lennox – who'd been told to wear out the Dunfermline defence with his constant running – won a corner. It was struck by Charlie Gallacher and met perfectly by Billy McNeill whose solid header famously clinched the cup – Stein's first trophy of many.

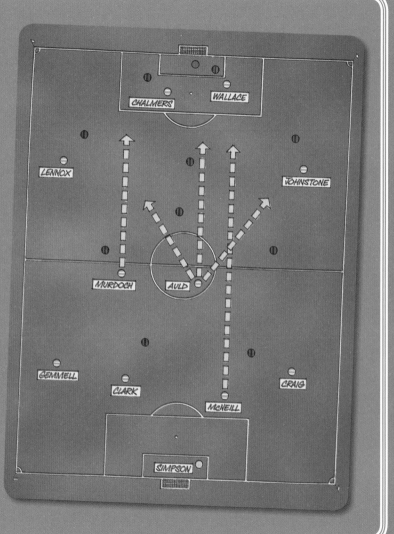

MCNEILL'S BIRTHDAY TREAT

Returning for a second spell as manager in the summer of 1987 – with the club on the cusp of its 100th year – Billy McNeill had a massive job on his hands to wrest the league championship back from Rangers. His clever use of on-field ploys made the most of his players' gifts and secured a centenary double.

On a pre-season tour of Sweden the manager and his assistant, Tommy Craig, carefully explained to the squad exactly what they should be doing regardless of whether or not they were in possession.

Without the ball they were told to press high up the field, 'defending from the front' in other words. If the opposition wanted room to walk the ball out of defence they would be met and immediately pressurised by Andy Walker and Frank McAvennie, with Tommy Burns and Joe Miller closing in from the wings.

McNeill had also spotted that teams in Scotland, at that time, tended to play in nothing other than a standard 4-4-2 formation. Why then were four defenders needed to nullify just two forwards? It would be better, he reckoned, to play with three central defenders, at least at home.

Two would mark the strikers while another, often Roy Aitken as captain, would remain spare to sweep up any loose balls, cover challenges and nullify bursts from midfield towards Pat Bonner's goal.

The major benefit of this tactic was that it freed two young full backs to rampage up and down the flanks at will. This, in effect, was what Chris Morris and Anton Rogan did all season long, supporting their wingers and turning the team into an irrepressible attacking force.

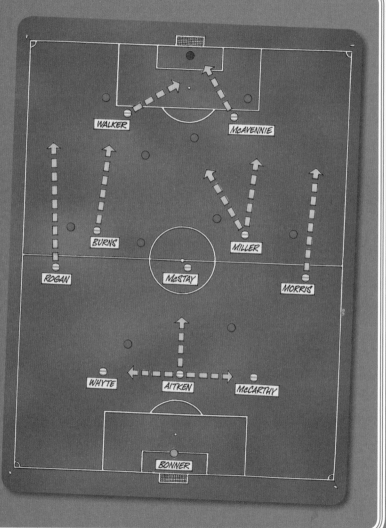

O'NEILL PACKS THE MIDFIELD

Martin O'Neill was one of a number of managers to favour a 3-5-2 system which was becoming fashionable at the beginning of this century. This was a style based around the high energy shuttling of the ball out of defence on the break. At its core there would be a powerful central midfield trio, supported by wing backs, who tended to be stationed higher up the pitch than traditional full backs.

On one flank there was Alan Thompson, a thoughtful and cultured player in possession of a superb left foot. On the right there was an out and out speed merchant – the quiet but deadly Frenchman Didier Agathe – who would leave opponents trailing as he burst towards the by-line.

A clear signal of how the manager intended to play was the signing of Neil Lennon in Dec 2000. A holding midfielder supreme, he'd augment a role already being carried out by Paul Lambert who'd won the Champions League with Borussia Dortmund. This central pairing also allowed the young Bulgarian star, Stiliyan Petrov, to roam slightly farther forward in support of the strikers.

Taken together as a five slung across the middle of the park, they acted both as a screen for the defence and the creative hub of the chances developed for Chris Sutton and Henrik Larsson in attack.

O'Neill also tended to favour larger-than-life Herculean defenders. The emphasis was not so much on speed but blocking the route to goal with full-blooded brawn. It was not always the prettiest way to play but Joos Valgaeren, Johan Mjallby and the man-mountain Bobo Balde ended up on the winning side more often than not during their time in the Hoops.

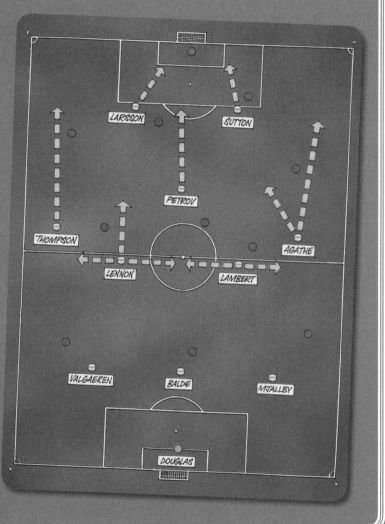

LARSSON

SUTTON

THOMPSON

PETROV

AGATHE

LENNON

LAMBERT

VALGAEREN

BALDE

MJALLBY

DOUGLAS

**GREAT
GAFFERS**

When one individual manages a club
for approaching half a century he's bound to leave his mark. Willie Maley did much more than that. As Celtic's first boss he was the driving force behind 30 major trophy victories over 43 years, a dazzling haul of 16 league titles and 14 Scottish Cups.

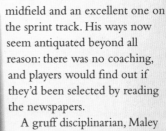

He'd been appointed 'Secretary-Manager' at the age of 29, in 1897, after a decent career in Celtic's midfield and an excellent one on the sprint track. His ways now seem antiquated beyond all reason: there was no coaching, and players would find out if they'd been selected by reading the newspapers.

A gruff disciplinarian, Maley could terrorise even the most experienced professional simply by glaring in their direction. It is therefore an oddity that such a stoic would send out teams which thrilled crowds with their neat passing and cavalier approach. Maley's real gift was an ability to spot talented youngsters such as Lyon,

Jock Stein, perhaps the greatest manager of them all

Buchan, Quinn and McNair. Over successive eras he created three near-untouchable teams, almost entirely from scratch.

Aged 72 when he was coaxed into retirement in 1940, a tear was said to have welled in the old man's eye as chairman Tom White paid this tribute: "The history of Celtic is indissolubly the story of Willie Maley."

Billy McNeill takes a bow after the 1988 Scottish Cup final victory

'Hard act to follow' doesn't do justice to the task facing his successor, Jimmy McStay. The Hoops' former centre half had done well at Alloa, but was said to be too nice to succeed back at Parkhead. His chances were also hampered by constant meddling from the boardroom. After five threadbare wartime seasons he was replaced, in 1945, by Jimmy McGrory.

It was hoped that the great striker's magic would rub off on his teams. But McGrory too had a quiet and deferential nature which allowed the board to

Tommy Burns couldn't quite take the club back to the top...

throw their weight around. Even though he remained at the helm for 20 years Celtic were little more than cup specialists. So in 1965 action was finally taken to bring back the glory days; McGrory made way for Jock Stein and things would never be the same again.

Stein coached the players day-in, day-out and he alone picked the team. Six weeks after taking charge he'd secured the Scottish Cup – Celtic's first trophy in eight years. It was the beginning of an age in which his sides smashed every record in the book, winning cups and titles with unnerving regularity.

His fine-tuned brand of attacking football also catapulted Celtic to the highest position in the continental game. This was never more so than in the destruction of Inter Milan during the European Cup final of 1967.

Having "saved Celtic", as Bobby Murdoch once put it, Big Jock was involved in a serious car crash in 1975 which weakened him. Three years later another former captain, Billy McNeill, took over.

This seemed like a natural progression and so it proved when the league was won on the final day of his first season, against Rangers. McNeill's side also made advances in Europe, beating Ajax and giving

Real Madrid an almighty scare in the latter stages of the European Cup.

Frustratingly, a deterioration in relations with the board led to a parting of the ways in 1983, but he would remain the king in exile throughout Davie Hay's four year tenure.

Another quiet man, Hay fought valiantly against the New Firm of Aberdeen and Dundee United – and then a resurgent Rangers – before McNeill was ushered back for the centenary season in the spring of 1987.

Having overseen a vast reconstruction job on the team, there was delight at securing an unexpected league and cup double in the club's 100th year. This was to be the high watermark of McNeill's second spell. Lack of serious investment left the manager stripped of the tools needed to compete against a

... but Wim Jansen, seen here celebrating the 1998 league title with Murdo MacLeod, did

Inspirational genius
Martin O'Neill with the
2001 Scottish Cup

financially superior Ibrox outfit.

By 1991, when Liam Brady took over, Celtic were heading into a long trophyless slough of despond. After just two seasons the pressures of the job forced the Irishman out and he was followed through the exit door in 1994 by Lou Macari.

There were high hopes for the next gaffer – Tommy Burns. Alas, having won the Scottish Cup in 1995 he was not quite able to break Rangers' stranglehold on the title. That honour fell to a little poodle-haired Dutchman by the name of Wim Jansen. Having thwarted the Gers dream of ten titles on the bounce Jansen left before the celebratory champagne had lost its fizz.

His place was taken by Dr Jozef Venglos and then, in 1999, there followed the ill-starred eight-month reign of John Barnes. The inexperienced Englishman was totally out of his depth and after a desperate Scottish Cup defeat at home to Inverness Caledonian Thistle the only way was up; the coming of Martin O'Neill meant that the trajectory would be stratospheric.

After informing the fans, in June 2000, that his father had once told him to "walk to Glasgow" if ever offered the Celtic job, he wasted no time in confirming his reputation as an inspirational genius of a coach.

Rangers, the champions, were obliterated 6-2 that August in the first great high of many in a treble-winning season. Over the next five years there would be league titles, domestic cups, Champions League victories and an unforgettable run to the UEFA Cup final.

'The Blessed Martin' departed to care for his sick wife in 2005, leaving Gordon Strachan to build on his legacy at home and abroad by taking three successive titles and reaching the last 16 of Europe's premier tournament. He was not everyone's cup of tea, but he was effective.

Tony Mowbray took charge for the 2009/10 campaign but never got into top gear. By spring the team were out of the championship race and a dreadful 4-0 defeat to St Mirren meant the hunt would begin again for the man who'd keep Celtic where Maley, Stein and the others from days of yore would have demanded they be — at the top.

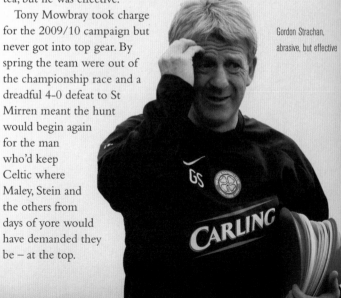

Gordon Strachan, abrasive, but effective

MEMORABLE
MATCHES

CELTIC 7 RANGERS 1

League Cup final, Hampden Park, Glasgow, 19th October 1957

More than half a century after this game was played the scoreline remains the biggest beating ever handed out by one Old Firm side to another. It was a day when several talented players in green and white made the most of their gifts, in an era of relative poverty for Celtic.

Willie Fernie was head and shoulders above the rest that mild afternoon; voted man of the match for his powerful running and control of the play from right half. Fernie's performance inspired others such as Neilly Mochan, Bobby Collins, Billy McPhail and the evergreen Charlie Tully.

Before kick-off the players had taken the impromptu decision to focus their energies on playing through the middle, rather than the wings. The idea was to overpower the Rangers' defence on the ground and in the air.

It worked, with Celtic's nimble forwards running their opponents ragged. In particular John Valentine, Rangers' centre half, was unable to get to grips with Celtic's tempo and rhythm.

Collins and Tully had both hit the crossbar before

Sammy Wilson opened the scoring in the 23rd minute. Mochan then made it two with a fizzing shot from a tight angle on the stroke of half time.

Rangers were already demoralised, but would be humiliated by

teatime. McPhail headed home on 53 minutes to put his team 3-0 ahead. Rangers got one back before McPhail scored another with a quarter of the match left. Shortly afterwards Mochan notched his second on the volley.

Rangers keeper George Niven makes a rare save in a match in which he conceded seven!

McPhail then went on to secure his hat-trick and Fernie capped off a wondrous display with a last-minute penalty to make it 7-1.

Sean Fallon, who played at full back, admitted they'd had one of those golden days when everyone was in top gear: "We never expected to win by such a margin but as the game progressed the confidence grew sky-high. Everything clicked and it seemed we couldn't do anything wrong. It was unbelievable."

There would be no more trophies until the middle of the next decade, but still the memories of 'Hampden in Sun – Celtic 7 Rangers 1' would be a source of pride for many long years to come.

Celtic:
Beattie, Donnelly, Fallon, Fernie, Evans, Peacock, Tully, Collins, McPhail, Wilson, Mochan

Scorer:
Wilson, Mochan (2), McPhail (3), Fernie

Attendance:
82,000

CELTIC 2 INTERNAZIONALE 1

European Cup final, Estadio Nacional, Lisbon, 25th May, 1967

Celtic's finest hour and a half came in a Romanesque amphitheatre on the outskirts of Lisbon. Thousands travelled to support them, including a convoy of cars dubbed The Celticade. Schools and workplaces emptied early at home so people could huddle around their black and white TV's to follow the drama.

They watched a nightmare opening when, after just eight minutes, Jim Craig was adjudged to have brought down Cappellini inside the box. It's a moment he remembers all too well: "I made slight contact with my right leg and, all credit to him, he made a very good job of crashing to the ground." The resulting penalty sent Simpson the wrong way and Inter into the lead.

Celtic dominated the rest of the half, coming close on several occasions, without actually breaching the Italians' defence. Billy McNeill recalls the dearth of action at his end of the field: "Once Inter scored John Clark and I could have gone and sat in the stand for all we were needed."

In the dressing room they were soothed by their manager, who told them to be patient, keep playing as they were, but make more effort to cut balls back into space from the wings.

Over the next 45 minutes Inter were pulverised, with Sarti in goal being forced into a series of scrambled saves. For a time it looked as though Celtic would be kept out by the stifling Catenaccio padlock, an ugly defensive tool so loved by Inter's boss, Helenio Herrera.

Eventually the Italians wilted under intense pressure. First Tommy Gemmell rampaged up from the back in typical style to thump a shot home; then with just six minutes remaining Murdoch hit a left-foot drive which was turned in at close range by Steve Chalmers.

Celtic had reached the highest high and struck a blow for football itself. Jock Stein said that the team would "never be beaten" but perhaps the importance of their success was best summed up by one French magazine which exclaimed: "Never has a victory been more warmly welcomed, nor a winning goal been greeted with such an explosion of joy throughout the continent."

Keeper Ronnie Simpson claims the ball as Inter forwards lurk

Celtic:
Simpson, Craig, Gemmell, Murdoch, McNeill, Clark, Johnstone, Wallace, Chalmers, Auld, Lennox, (Fallon gk not used)

Scorer:
Gemmell, Chalmers

Attendance:
45,000

CELTIC 4 RANGERS 2

Scottish Premier League, Celtic Park, Glasgow, 21st May 1979

The last Old Firm encounter of Billy McNeill's first season as manager had been postponed from January due to severe winter weather. It was the final game of the Hoops' season and saw the two clubs locked at the top of the table in a high wire fight for the championship which would ultimately be decided by 90 minutes of unforgettable Monday night action.

George Mcluskey got Celtic's second

Celtic knew that a win would make them champions, while a draw or a defeat meant their old adversaries could pip them by winning games in hand elsewhere.

Things started well for Rangers who scored after nine minutes and held that lead until half time.

It looked even more likely that the title would be going to Ibrox when, ten minutes after the break, Johnny Doyle – in sheer frustration – booted Rangers' Alex McDonald as he lay on the ground. Doyle was ordered off, reducing Celtic to ten men.

Two things then swung the game in their favour; the frenzied backing of the home support and Roy Aitken's absolute will to win.

It was Aitken himself who produced the equaliser on 67 minutes. Shortly after that George McCluskey got a second, before Rangers equalised.

It was all or nothing now and with just seven minutes left the Gers contrived to score an own goal as Celtic poured forward. The tension had reached breaking point – any slip-ups and the league was gone. Celtic's by-kicks and throw-ins were cheered as if they were goals and then, with seconds remaining, Murdo MacLeod settled things, arrowing in a screamer from 20 yards.

The cry went up from The Jungle: "We've Won the League Again - Fly the Flag." It would come to be known, of course, as the night Ten Men Won The League.

On the pitch the players cavorted and sang in front of the fans and for the man of the match, Roy Aitken, it was "far and away the best game I have ever played in."

Later the club's chairman, Desmond White, described it as "the finest night since Lisbon."

Roy Aitken: "The best game I ever played in"

Celtic:
Latchford, McGrain, Lynch, Aitken, McAdam, Edvaldsson, Provan, Conroy (Lennox), McCluskey, MacLeod, Doyle

Scorer:
Aitken, McCluskey, Jackson (og), MacLeod

Attendance:
60,000

CELTIC 2 DUNDEE UNITED 1

Scottish Cup final, Hampden Park, Glasgow, 14th May 1988

This match gave Celtic the chance of doing the double in their centenary year. Flair and consistency had seen them confound the experts who'd predicted Rangers would be the dominant outfit even before a ball had been kicked that season.

Billy McNeill was back at the helm and had brought in Frank McAvennie, from West Ham, and Andy Walker. The duo's goals helped win the league. Now they had to get the better of Dundee United who'd reached the UEFA Cup final the previous season.

Just before kick-off it emerged that Peter Grant had failed to recover from a broken foot; while Pat Bonner had picked up an injury in training and was unable to take his place in goal.

Still, it was one of those classic cup final afternoons, blue skies and warm sun, a festival atmosphere and a bumper crowd. Even the appearance of controversial Prime Minister Maggie Thatcher failed to take the gloss off the occasion.

The first-half stuttered along with neither side really on top. Then, four minutes into the second 45, United's Kevin Gallacher burst through to crash a shot past stand-in goalie Allen McKnight. Celtic's captain, Roy Aitken, steeled himself for yet another comeback in a season when so many had been successfully mounted. "We had lost one goal, now we had to go and score two," he says.

On and on they pressed, with their opponents dropping ever deeper into defence. Then the manager brought on two experienced subs, Mark McGhee and Billy Stark, to give added purpose to the attack. The double switch paid off when McAvennie headed in from close range with 15 minutes left.

Typically this Celtic side – like the best of years gone by – were not prepared to settle for a draw in normal time. Having scored once the striker urged his team-mates to go and "get the winner." Sure enough that came, from the boot of the same player, with just seconds to play.

The fans had the birthday present they so desired and McNeill, the man who'd turned the team around, knew the importance of the achievement, saying: "There's a fairytale about this club and it's almost as if it has come true once again."

Celtic:
McKnight,
Morris, McCarthy,
Whyte (Stark),
Rogan,
Miller, Aitken,
McStay, Burns,
McAvennie,
Walker
(McGhee)

Scorer:
McAvennie (2)

Attendance:
74,000

CELTIC COMIC STRIP HISTORY 4

1960... AND CELTIC WERE TRAVELLING TO AIRDRIE FOR A LEAGUE MATCH. SEEING A FAMILIAR FIGURE STANDING BY THE SIDE OF THE ROAD, CHAIRMAN ROBERT KELLY STOPPED THE COACH...

AREN'T YOU OUR RESERVE 'KEEPER?

YES, SIR — WILLIE GOLDIE. I'M WAITING FOR A LIFT... ON MY WAY TO WATCH THE GAME...

THEN JUMP ON!

THE ALL-POWERFUL CELTIC CHAIRMAN WAS IMPRESSED BY GOLDIE'S LOYALTY.

YOU WON'T JUST BE WATCHING TODAY... YOU'LL BE PLAYING!

PLAYING? IN GOAL?

SADLY, IT PROVED TO BE A MISTAKE...

CELTIC LOST 0-2, AND THE STAND-IN GOALIE WAS TO BLAME FOR BOTH GOALS. HE **NEVER** PLAYED FOR THE CLUB AGAIN.

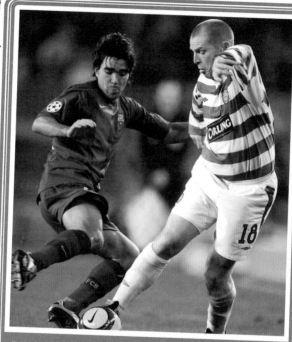

IF YOU KNOW YOUR HISTORY
REBELLION AND RENEWAL
1992-2010

A fixture pile-up caused by the hard winter of 1978/79 gave Celtic time to settle under Billy McNeill's stewardship. By May they had the chance to secure the league title with a victory against Rangers at Parkhead. This would turn out to be one of the most memorable nights in the club's post-war history – a 4-2 win with just ten men.

Danny McGrain and Murdo MacLeod try to close down Real Madrid's Laurie Cunningham in the 1980 European Cup

However, the 1980s brought a new reality: they were no longer capable of competing at the very top in Europe and the conveyor belt of brilliant youngsters had slowed considerably. There was also a threat from Dundee United and Aberdeen, with both those sides at their strongest for generations.

The Bhoys reached the quarter-finals of the European Cup in 1980, losing narrowly to Real

Madrid. This defeat shook their confidence in the final weeks of the season, allowing Aberdeen to take the title. The Scottish Cup final provided a silver-lining, though the victory over Rangers was marred by a full-scale riot on the pitch at full time.

The team was given a lift by the emergence of Charlie Nicholas during the next campaign, a youngster described by his manager as "a special player." Nicholas and Frank McGarvey struck up an effective partnership and propelled Celtic to their 33rd league title.

Champagne Charlie added fizz in the early 1980s

Yet behind the scenes relations between Billy McNeill and the directors were beginning to sour, mainly over money. On top of that Nicholas sustained a broken leg in the 1981/82 campaign and Johnny Doyle, a popular winger, died in an electrical accident. However, the championship was retained on the final day of the league programme.

The League Cup was won – at Rangers' expense –

Frank McAvennie celebrates the centenary Double in the sun at Hampden in 1988

the season after that, but things were destabilised in the Premier Division by rumours that Nicholas was preparing for a move to England. Frustratingly he did indeed depart, to Arsenal, in the summer of 1983. What had not been expected was that McNeill would follow him south, to Manchester City, his relations with the board having passed the point of no return.

Davie Hay, a relatively inexperienced coach, stepped into the breach. It was another difficult period, with his side finishing second in each of the domestic competitions in 1984. Hay bagged the Scottish Cup at the end of the next campaign thanks to a comeback triggered by Davie Provan. His sublime, curling free kick at Hampden having what the player remembered as a "devastating effect" on Dundee United who rightly feared a traditional Celtic surge to glory in the closing minutes.

There was further progress when the title was unexpectedly snatched from Hearts on the closing day of the 1985/86 season. Yet when Rangers won the league under Graeme Souness 12 months later, Billy McNeill was dramatically brought back from England. It was a move which brought instant success, with a fine league and cup double being won in Celtic's centenary year of 1988.

When the Scottish Cup was retained a year later in a hard-fought Old Firm final, it looked as though the 'Rangers Revolution' was faltering. Sadly it was a former hero who destroyed that notion as Mo Johnston astonished the football world by turning his back on a proposed return to Parkhead to sign instead for Rangers.

The affair shook Celtic badly and they were unable to keep pace financially with their old foes. In 1991 Billy McNeill lost his job, the result of two seasons without a trophy. This came as various factions – the fans, the board and a group of 'rebel' businessmen –

fought to decide the future direction of the club. That
battle was won in March 1994 by the diminutive
Scots-Canadian, Fergus McCann.

On the field Rangers remained rampant, while
Celtic were unable even to beat Raith Rovers in the
League Cup final of 1994. There were signs of
regeneration elsewhere however, as McCann's five
year plan to transform the club bore fruit. After a
season based at Hampden an impressive new
north stand emerged at Parkhead. Also, in that
same summer of 1995, The Hoops

brought a run of six years without a trophy to an
end by beating Airdrie to the Scottish Cup.

Tommy Burns, in his first year in charge, was
delighted by the victory but admitted afterwards that
his relationship with McCann "was not as it should
be." Ultimately it was the chairman who won their
battle of wills, removing Burns in 1997 after he'd
come extremely close to stopping
Rangers winning their ninth
successive championship.

Champions again in
1998 ater a 2-0 win
over St Johnstone

CLUB 1888

Henrik Larsson was recruited by Wim Jansen and became a modern legend

His replacement, Wim Jansen, arrived from the Netherlands with a Swedish striker called Henrik Larsson in tow. First his side took the League Cup and then stopped the rot by regaining the title, ten years after The Hoops were last champions. Jansen walked away shortly afterwards and another two years of turmoil were endured before Celtic appointed the man capable of offering more than mere fleeting glory.

Martin O'Neill promised to "do everything I possibly can to bring some success to this football club."

He was as good as his word – winning the treble in his first season, re-establishing Celtic as a European force and putting Rangers well and truly in the shade for the bulk of his unforgettable five years in charge.

When Gordon Strachan took over in 2005 Celtic were in better shape than at any time since the mid-1970s. Strachan kept the team very much on top at home and oversaw some great European nights – such as victories over AC Milan and Manchester United – the latter of which he described as "priceless."

But his final season as boss – 2008/09 – ended on a low with Rangers champions once again. Celtic, with Tony Mowbray taking over the reins, were unable to capitalise on the poor financial state of affairs at Ibrox and allowed Walter Smith's men to canter to another title. Once again the 'grand old team' of Glasgow's east end was facing adversity; it had been that way throughout Celtic's long and illustrious story but as always they were ready to play their way back to the top again.

THE MEN WHO MADE CELTIC

One man dominates the history of Celtic's formation. He was Andrew Kerins – commonly known today as Brother Walfrid, the name he took on becoming a monk in 1864.

Like so many others he'd come to the west of Scotland from Ireland during the bleak years which followed the great hunger of the mid-19th century, only to encounter malnourishment, squalor and disease; conditions which were little better than those he'd left behind.

The direction of his life changed when he decided to train as a teacher through the Marist Order, which was committed to providing education for the poor. Eventually Walfrid became headmaster at the Sacred Heart School in Glasgow's east end and placed himself at the very centre of life in the area.

With his friend and colleague, Brother Dorotheus, he helped found a 'penny dinner' charity which allowed parents to feed their children for a nominal sum, thus appearing to avoid the indignity of relying on handouts. This was, in his own words, "a very great blessing".

Then, having seen how thousands were prepared to

Andrew Kerins, aka Brother Walfrid, saw football as a way of bonding a community…

152

watch Hibs play against a local
team called Renton, Walfrid
rightly concluded that football
could be extremely useful to
his fundraising activities. It
would also foster pride in being
Catholic and Irish in Glasgow
and keep people of that
background together and out
of the rival soup kitchens that
were being provided by the
Presbyterian churches.

...in a time in
which Glasgow's
Catholics lived in
poor conditions

By early 1887 he began
seeking support for the new
venture, only to discover
he was pushing at an open
door. The neighbouring parishes of St Andrew's and St
Alphonsus's helped his own – St Mary's – in bringing
matters to a head. Using their contacts they enlisted
other important figures in Catholic circles, not churchmen
but community organisers and politicians.

Most prominent among these was John Glass – a
man commonly felt to have been instrumental in turning
Walfrid's dream into reality. He was a builder by trade
and known for his work with the Catholic Union and in
particular the Home Government Branch of the United
Irish League.

Home Rule for Ireland was one of the burning issues
of the day and Glass helped to organise several rallies
at which the notable republican Michael Davitt spoke –

addressing the Highland Scots on topics such as land reform. Davitt himself became an honorary Celtic patron, having laid a shamrock-sprinkled sod of grass in the centre circle at Parkhead.

There's little doubt Glass's political views were shared by the vast majority of those who would become supporters of the club. He was, in essence, Walfrid's right hand man – chairing the meeting at which Celtic was constituted. His Liberalism ensured it would be an outward looking and non-sectarian institution.

However, he was crucial for another reason. Glass's solid, practical nature drove things forward and, having been put in charge of recruitment, he managed to secure some of the finest players in Scotland, including James Kelly of Renton. Kelly himself was also an Irish Home Ruler and would go on to be a director whose family held a place on the board until 1994.

This was an audacious signing, one which ensured Celtic's growth as a force in the game. Glass said that Celtic may have "fizzled out" without their inspirational centre half. It could have been, as one newspaper put it at the time, a case of 'No Kelly, No Kel-tic!'

Others with potential had been spotted by Glass and Walfrid – notably the brothers Tom and Willie Maley, both of whom played in the inaugural victory over Rangers. They were talked into a role by Glass's persuasive tongue. Tom would become a director and a highly energised committee man, while his brother Willie spent an incredible 43 years as Celtic's manager – one of the most influential figures in the entire history of the club.

Other men of high standing put their names forward at the outset. His Grace the Archbishop of Glasgow, Charles Eyre, was listed as a patron, stumping up 20 shillings for the privilege (even though he'd shown little interest in football until that point). The same amount came from two dozen others, including Dr John Conway, a much respected and loved GP who turned his back on a comfortable middle-class existence to practice medicine among the poor. A member of the Royal College of Physicians, he was chairman for the first two years before Glass himself took over. Essentially these were men of principle who'd understood the huge possibilities offered by Walfrid's venture. They lived in an age of industrial and social upheaval, but one in which it was possible to effect lasting change. Their commitment and hard work did not go unrewarded; Celtic will forever stand as their legacy.

Willie Maley, who spent an incredible 43 years as Celtic's manager

HONOURS AND RECORDS

MAJOR HONOURS

WINNERS

European Cup 1967

Scottish League 1893, 1894, 1896, 1898, 1905, 1906, 1907, 1908, 1909, 1910, 1914, 1915, 1916, 1917, 1919, 1922, 1926, 1936, 1938, 1954, 1966, 1967, 1968, 1969, 1970, 1971, 1972, 1973, 1974, 1977, 1979, 1981, 1982, 1986, 1988, 1998, 2001, 2002, 2004, 2006, 2007, 2008

Scottish Cup 1892, 1899, 1900, 1904, 1907, 1908, 1911, 1912, 1914, 1923, 1925, 1927, 1931, 1933, 1937, 1951, 1954, 1965, **1967, 1969, 1971, 1972, 1974, 1975, 1977, 1980, 1985, 1988, 1989, 1995, 2001, 2004, 2005, 2007**

Scottish League Cup 1957, 1958, 1966, 1967, 1968, 1969, 1970, 1975, 1983, 1998, 2000, 2001, 2006, 2009

International Exhibition Cup 1902

Coronation Cup 1953

RUNNERS-UP
European Cup 1970
UEFA Cup 2003
World Club Championship 1967

MINOR HONOURS

**Glasgow Cup 1891, 1892, 1895,
1896, 1905, 1906, 1907, 1908,
1910, 1916, 1917, 1920, 1921,
1927, 1928, 1929, 1931, 1939,
1941, 1949, 1956, 1962, 1964,
1965, 1967, 1986, 1970, 1975,
1982**
Charity Cup 1892, 1894, 1895,
1896, 1899, 1903, 1905, 1908,
1912, 1913, 1914, 1915, 1916,
1917, 1918, 1920, 1921, 1924,
1926, 1936, 1937, 1938, 1943,
1950, 1953, 1959, 1961* (shared
with Clyde)
Ferençvaros Vase 1914
Navy and Army War Fund
Shield 1918
Empire Exhibition Trophy 1938
Victory in Europe Cup 1945
St Mungo's Cup 1951
CNE Cup 1968
Drybrough Cup 1974
World of Soccer Cup 1977
Feyenoord Tournament 1981
London Evening Standard 5-a-side
Trophy 1981
Dubai Champions Cup 1989
Tennents' Sixes 1992
**Jock Stein Friendship Cup 2008,
2009**
Translink Cup 2009
Wembley Cup 2009

BBC Sports Personality of the Year,
Team Award 1967
**France Football, European Team
of the Year 1970**
FIFA Fair Play Award 2003
DB UEFA Award 2003

RECORDS
CLUB RECORDS
Record victory: 11-0 v Dundee, 26th
Oct 1895
**Record defeat: 0-8 v Motherwell,
30th April 1937**
Highest home attendance: 92,000 v
Rangers, 1st Jan 1938
**Scottish League record
attendance: Rangers v Celtic,
118,567, 2nd Jan 1939**
European club match record
attendance: 146,433 v Aberdeen,
Scottish Cup final, Hampden Park,
24th April 1937
**European Cup record attendance:
135,826 v Leeds Utd, European
Cup semi-final, Hampden Park,
15th April 1970**
Longest run without defeat in the
Scottish League: 1915, won 49 and
drew 13 matches between 13th Nov
1915 and 21st April 1917
**Longest winning league run: 25 in
2003/04**
Highest points total in a season:
103 in 2001/02
Most League wins: 33 in 2001/02
Most home wins: 19 in 1921/22
Most away wins: 17 in 1915/16
Fewest home defeats: 0, 21 times

Fewest away defeats: 0, 4 times
Lowest points total: 21 in 1890/91
Most defeats: 15 in 1947/48 and 1977/78
Most goals scored: 116 in 1915/16
Fewest goals conceded: 13 in 1897/98

INDIVIDUAL RECORDS

Highest individual goals in a single season: Henrik Larsson, 53, 2000/01
Highest total goals for Celtic: Jimmy McGrory, 529, 1922-38
Most goals in a league match: Jimmy McGrory, 8 v Dunfermline, 14th Jan 1928
Record total Celtic appearances: Billy McNeill, 790
Record Scottish league appearances: Alec McNair, 583, 1905-1925
Record European appearances: Billy McNeill, 69, 1963-1975
Most capped player: Paul McStay, 76 (right)

SCOTTISH PFA PLAYER OF THE YEAR

1980 Davie Provan
1983 Charlie Nicholas
1987 Brian McClair
1988 Paul McStay
1990 Paul Elliott
1997 Paulo di Canio
1998 Jackie McNamara
1999 Henrik Larsson
2000 Mark Viduka
2001 Henrik Larsson
2004 Chris Sutton
2005 John Hartson
2006 Sean Maloney
2007 Shunsuke Nakamura
2008 Aiden McGeady
2009 Scott Brown

SCOTTISH FOOTBALL WRITERS PLAYER OF THE YEAR

1965 Billy McNeill
1967 Ronnie Simpson
1969 Bobby Murdoch
1973 George Connelly
1977 Danny McGrain
1983 Charlie Nicholas
1987 Brian McClair
1988 Paul McStay
1998 Craig Burley
1999 Henrik Larsson
2001 Henrik Larsson
2002 Paul Lambert
2004 Jackie McNamara
2005 John Hartson
2007 Shunsuke Nakamura
2009 Gary Caldwell

FIRSTS AND LASTS

- First Scottish club to win nine Championships in a row. When Celtic did this – between 1966 and 1974 – they held the joint world record for consecutive success in domestic titles.
- **First British club to reach the European Cup final, 1967**
- First northern European club to win the European Cup, 1967

- Only Scottish and first British club to win the European Cup, 1967
- Highest score in a domestic cup final: 7-1 v Rangers, 1957
- **World record for successive appearances in the final of a major competition, with 14 Consecutive League Cup finals between 1965-1978**
- Fastest hat-trick in European club football: Mark Burchill v Jeunesse Esch, 2002/03
- **Earliest date to win SPL Championship (twice with six games remaining) v Kilmarnock 18th April 2004, Hearts 5th April 2006**
- Biggest margin of victory in SPL: 8-1 v Dunfermline, 19th Feb 2006 & v St Mirren 7-0, 28th Feb 2009
- **Longest unbeaten home record by Scottish club: 22nd Aug 2001 to 21st April 2004 – 77 matches**
- Record transfer fee for a player between Scottish clubs: £4.4 million to Hibs for Scott Brown, 16th May 2007
- **First weekly club newspaper in the UK: *The Celtic View*, 1965**